CHRONICLES OF
HICKORY COUNTY

CHRONICLES OF HICKORY COUNTY

BILLY PEARSON

ISBN: 1515202534
ISBN 13: 9781515202530

PREFIX

Most of the name of places in our region of the state as in a lot of other places come from the early French explorers. Ozarks name come from words AUX-ARC.

In 1955, I was enrolled in department of agriculture at Missouri University. We had a professor by the name of Allen Purdy. In our first class we had to tell where we were from and our name. Things were going very nice until it came to this very large hunky fellow and he was from Ava. Mr. Purdy said "Oh! You are a hillbilly." This young man jumped up and said "Hell no! That's them Arkansaws!" with this story I'm trying to make my point, we are slowly losing our Ozark slang and so are other regions. At that time in history I dated a girl from Alabama. I had to listen very carefully to understand her. Then my uncle married a lady from Kentucky. Twenty years later she still had that same southern accent. My wife was in St. Mary's Hospital in Rochester, Minnesota. Her roommate lived in the finger of Michigan. Sometimes we had to ask her to repeat what she had said. They also had trouble understanding us.

In a doctor's office at the Mayo Clinic, my wife said to the nurse "boy you people sure do talk funny" she shot right back "no honey it's you people who talk funny." With that said she asked if we were from the Ozarks of Missouri. Dumbfounded we said yes. After that exchange with the nurse we became very good friends.

HICKORY COUNTY HISTORY

This is written by Billy Pearson, information from individual sources and Hickory County Library.

CHRONICLES OF HICKORY COUNTY

INTRODUCTION

Originally, I started this book to make a few notes about the history of Hickory County, Missouri, based on what I have been told by my grandfather and uncle Ott who lived with my folks many years. I'm sure there are some mistakes. My intentions are not the alter the names or conceptions of anyone. I am writing this by what I have been told as well as the research from the Hickory County Library. I used names only when I believed it was necessary punctuate the story of the history. I have thoroughly read both books on Plainville U.S.A. which has given me more insight on how things were in the 1800s as Mr. West saw them.

I may be old as dirt, but not that old. I am amongst the oldest living resident of the county. I have lived here my entire life except for the short time I was going to M.U. During this time, I came home every weekend to my life's dream and also helping my parents on our farm.

I am a history nut and so is my grandson. Over the past several years, I have written several pages of family history and my family has enjoyed reading these writings very much. With the research I have conducted, along with the testimonies I have witnessed, I will try to be honest and fair to history of our little county. There are some repeats of information but was left this way as not to dismiss anything that might be missed. During my writing process, I felt it was important to gather facts accurately.

I've tried to write some of the history in story form where it could be written that way. Several stories of history could not be recorded because of unethical words to describe the event. We have also tried to write in telling a story of the history plus humor. Without a smile or laugh life would be dull. The bringing Hickory County from beginning to date is anything but dull.

I am sorry if I have offended anyone, this was not my intention.

Thank you and my GOD bless you.

1830	John Stark on Stark's Creek (Wilson p. 153); Sam Judy at Judy's Gap; J.C. Montgomery north of Wheatland.
1832	Zumwalts and Ingleses settled on Lindley Creek (Goodspeed p. 215)
1833	Antioch Primitive Baptist church organized. James Richardson and Elijah Williams, ministers. (Lay p. 12)
1834	Wax sealed letter from John West to Wm. Montgomery, Little Niangua, Missouri. (Wilso p. 139)
1835	Boonville to Springfield "old road" cut out. (Lay p. 10) Land West of Pomme de Terre River opened to whites. (Lay p. 12)
1836	Emigration and cheap money
1837	Financial panic. Alfred Lindsey settled south of Hermitage.
1838	First land entered by twelve parties. (Goodspeed p. 221)
1839	Land entered by Runyan, Malock, Kerchival, Vestal, Taylor, McCarroll, Owings, Mitchell, Farmer, Bryans, Henderson, McCracken, Arbuckle, Bradley, Blue, Ball, Whitehead, Chessur, Clardy families.
1840	Slicker War began at Judy's Gap. (Lay p. 39)
1841	Land entries by I.M. Cruce, Nathan Boswell, S.W. Harris, Aaron Yarnell.
1842	Land entries by Eliza Ingles, Jonas Brown, Ephraim Jamison, A. C. Nowell, Joseph Edde.
1843	Antioch Christian Church organized. M.Y. Pitts, Minister.
1844	Mastodon skeleton (20,000 year old) discovered near Avery (1839) sold to British Museum. W.S. Pickett Settled near Cross Timbers.

1845	Hickory County formed from parts of Benton and Polk counties. First meeting of County Court met in a newly erected crib or stable at Judge Joel B. Halbert's. Members: Amos Lindsey, Joel Halbert and Thomas Davis. County Taxes for the year $ 383.65.
1846	Second meeting of the county court met a Heard's spring one half mile north of Wheatland at the John Heard residence.
1847	Hermitage platted. Jacob A. Romans, County Seat Commissioner.
1848	Courthouse built at Hermitage. Quincy platted.
1849	Gold rush to California. First probate court in the county. Aaron Triplett first probate judge.
1850	W.F. Bradley, presiding judge of county court. County population 2,329. W.B. Estes settled near Wheatland. Little Niangua Baptist church organized.
1851	Land entries by Josiah Brown, H.C. Butler, J.W. Huffman.
1852	Elkton Baptist church organized. Total county taxes $515.98. Courthouse burned. (Goodspeed p. 238)
1853	Micajah Turner and Martha Brookshire married December 26 by Asa Johnson, Justice of the Peace
1854	Dry year in Missouri. J.C. Berard settled at Quincy.
1856	Jonathan Chaney and Elizabeth Starkey married September 4, by minister Wm. Henderson. E.D. Blair settled at Hermitage.
1857	Financial panic. Preston platted.
1858	Great Comet. W.E. Dorman built a two story hotel at Hermitage and put up a dinner bell.
1859	Wm. Pippin and Margaret Bybee married April 28 by Joel Harlow, J.P.

1864	"Nearly 1,000 men connected with the armies—about equally divided" (Goodspeed p. 242)
1865	Civil War ended. Veterans return.
1866	Hermitage Lodge A.F. and A. M. No 288 chartered. Wollen mill established at Quincy.
1867	First county attorney, Charles Kroff.
1868	Capt. W. H. Liggett, School Commissioner. (Goodspeed p. 597)
1869	Pittsburg Baptist Church organized. Wheatland platted. Hermitage Enterprise first published; also Hickory County Mirror by Wm. Moore.
1870	Stone jail at Hermitage and Wheatland flourmill built.
1871	Pittsburg Baptist Church house built. Cross Timbers platted.
1872	First store at Weaubleau. Weaubleau Christian Institute organized by John Whitaker, founder.
1873	Weaubleau Christian College building completed.
1874	Dry year. Macedonia Baptist Church organized.
1875	Baptist annual meeting—W. W. Palmer, moderator; J. H. Stonecipher, preacher.
1876	Cross Timbers school house built. Swedes come to county. Election returns for Governor: Phelps (D) 403; Finklenburg (R) 627
1877	Swedish Baptist Church began near Almon.
1878	First Democratic Court since 1860. Vote for Congress, A. M. Lay (D) 308; A. Underwood (R) 439; James Boyd (Greenback) 393. (State Almanac 1879 p. 94)
1879	Cyclone unroofed jail and court house. Alexander Murphy began ten years service as county school commissioner. (Goodspeed p. 602)

1880	Weaubleau surveyed. Election for Congress: Philips (D) 464; Rice (Greenback R) 754. (Official Directory of MO, 1881p. 47) County population 7,387.
1881	Second court house burned. Hermitage Brick Church house built. (M. E. South)
1882	Weaubleau Baptist Church organized. Democrats elect George S. Selvidge as State Representative. Hill (R) elected Superintendent of Schools. (Official Directory of MO, 1882 p. 62)
1883	Pittsburg Annual Baptist Meeting—J. M. Russell, Moderator; L. J. Tatum, Clerk.
1884	First issue of The Index. Elections results: (R) 1963; (D) 626.
1885	Cross Timbers M. E. Church built. Two-story frame school house built in Wheatland.
1886	Seven hotels in Wheatland. G. A. R. organized at Hermitage. (Hickory County Democrat, 4-23-86)
1887	Hermitage School House built. Galmey Post Office established. Wheatland I.O.O.F. organized.
1888	Wheatland Union Church house built. Elkton Baptist church built. Clark School House. Ten doctors in the county.
1889	Twelve members of the Bar in Hickory County (Goodspeed p. 239). Four advertised at Hermitage (Index). Hickory County Bank organized at Hermitage with W. H. Liggett, President and James Vaughan, Cashier; capitalized at $5,000.
1890	Judge Ben L. Mallonee re-elected. Durnell Chapel Baptist church organized. County population 9,453.
1891	Iron bridge at Hermitage constructed at cost of $5,699. Preston steam flour mill built.

1892	Nemo Baptist Church house built. Wheatland Baptist church organized. Seven Christian churches reported in county.
1899	Hermitage Baptist Church and Preston M. P. Church built. Weaubleau Bank organized (capitalized at $5,000).
1900	Zenith reached in population, 9,985. Election: (R) 1,281; (D) 773. J.H. Jones in Wheatland revival.
1901	Dry year. Dr. B. F. Cox reported trip to Indian Territory and Oklahoma (Index 5-21-03). First Hickory County fair held.
1902	Hermitage Lodge I.O.O.F. No. 670 organized. Jordan steam flour mill built.
1903	Weaubleau flour mill erected. Hermitage Christian Church organized.
1904	Hermitage Lodge I.O.O.F. No. 670 organized. Jordan steam flour mill built.
1905	Weaubleau flour mill erected. Hermitage Christian Church organized.
1906	$15,000 fire at Hermitage. Citizens Bank organized, W. F. Coon, President.
1907	Hickory County Fair held August 27-30. Wilson's History of Hickory County published.
1908	Pittsburg mines re-opened
1909	M. N. Neilhardt wrote from Winona, MO. "Keep sending your paper to Weaubleau and I'll pay for it when I get ready even if it is not worth a darn. Wife says it is all right." Walter Coon's auto visits Hermitage Fair and steals the show. First automobile many had seen.
1910	The Index sponsored Piano Contest. Election: (R) 689.
1911	Center Baptist Church organized, Dallas Erickson, Pastor.

1912	Demonstration of Majestic Ranges for sale at Knight and Sons, Weaubleau. Election: (R) 730; (D) 421; Progressive 375; Socialist 57.
1913	Weaubleau Christian College approved by State normal; Fred Cooper, President. Spring School at Preston with Irl R. Chrisope, Principal. First High School building at Wheatland built.
1914	Young's High Flyer will fly at Hickory County Fair, August 25-28.
1915	Queen Incubators advertised (The Index 5-6-15). County Fair buildings burned.
1916	Rural Mail Carrier's Examination held at Wheatland. Many California letters to Paul Murphy, publisher of The Index (10-12-16).
1917	533 names registered in the county for the War Department (The Index 7-12-17
1918	United War Work Campaign. Influenza epidemic.
1919	County Conference of Sunday School workers at Wheatland, H. E. Shumate, President. Big fire at Wheatland.
1920	The Index purchased from Paul Murphy by U. Elmer Wilson. Republican Primary tallies 1,150 votes.
1921	Enclosed car, Ford Coupe, $595. Don Harryman, Wheatland, and Ashcroft Motor Co., Weaubleau, agents.
1922	Articles on Consolidated Schools published. New high school building at Hermitage. Primary election: (R) 2,307; (D) 305. Wheatland Christian Church dedicated; Dr. A. L. Fisher, Dr. A. S. Johnston, H. H. Rogers, leading donors.
1923	New Ford touring car advertised for $295, F.O.B. Detroit, by Parker Motor Co., Wheatland. The Index the only newspaper in the county.

1924	$2,000 fire at Hermitage. County to have 56 miles of graded graveled roads; 34.6 miles already built.
1925	Lead mines at Seed Tick Prospect near Cross Timbers. Mill Creek Co. selling shares for $10 each.
1933	Wet and Dry election: 260 Wet, 1088 Dry (The Index 8-24-33).
1934	CWA Women's Work, Dorothy Boiler, Director.
1935	Pave U.S. 54 Association formed. George H. Miller admitted to the Bar.
1936	Election: Landon-2,310, Roosevelt-904
1937	Permanents $1 to $5 at Ruth's Beauty Shoppe, Hermitage. Thirteen children from County at free Warsaw Clinic.
1938	Summer camp for Baptist girls at Gum Spring, June 14-16. Election: Caulfield (R) 1,149: Clark (D) 610.
1939	U.S. 54 paved. Terraces built on R.E. Tull farm. County Sunday School Convention at Hermitage July 2.
1940	U.S. 54 open through county. History of Draft Order numbers 637 (The Index 11-14-40). County population 6,506
1941	World War II began.
1942	War Relief Fund for Red Cross collects $473.78. AAA dinner at Brick Church (Hermitage). 9th anniversary of AAA.
1943	New marriage law explained. Ration Book 3 applications. War Fund Campaign collects $1,500.
1944	Soybeans for Hickory County recommended by County Agent L. W. Doran. Gerald Parsons awarded the Purple Heart.
1945	20,000 fish plated in Hickory County waters. Achievement Day Program for Extension clubs held September 29th.

1946	New Empire substation built east of Hermitage.
1947	Old age assistance totals $98, 290 for county. Monthly average $25.34. School lunch program.
1948	Balanced Farming Field Day at Floyd Pearson farm; 200 present. New buildings for County Fair. Owsley Pie Supper Proceeds--$163.60. Donald Shull, teacher.
1949	$75,000 fire at Hermitage. Loss of Lightfoot, Troxel, Pope, Dorman and Day buildings. County assessed valuation $4,706,286. Weaubleau Baptist and St. Bridget Catholic churches at Hermitage dedicated. World War I and II Memorial dedicated at Hermitage.
1950	County population 5,377. County Historical Society organized; Ralph Nevins, president.

Chapter 1

BILLY PEARSON

Start of the Organization We Now Call Hickory County

In the 1830's and before the land west of Pomme de Terre (land of the potato) river was Indian land. Whites were not permitted to settle here. The name of the river is translated for Indian language to French because of huge amount of a plant called by white man Jerusalem artichoke. The bulb on the bottom of the plant tasted like white man potato. It was one of the main food sources of the Indians who lived in this area.

The land was opened up to settlers in 1830. In 1829 John Jones crossed the river and staked out one hundred sixty acres. In order for the Jones family to survive, they had to be very tough and independent. They were hard working, law-abiding people who tried to do what was right. Until the mid-1800s, there was no law except your own. Only the very tough survived. The seventh generation is on this land as 2014. We are a tight-knit family and we are proud of our land that has been in our family for generations.

On April 14, 1845 state legislature approved the boundary lines of an area we now call Hickory County. The reason for a new county it took four days to drive to the county seat to do your business. The new county was formed mainly from Benton on the north and Polk on the south. The four day trip to the county seat was very dangerous because there were very little law to none, except your own. The roads were mostly trails at that time very difficult to get a wagon through. This was brought about by a group of citizens had petition the Governor for a county seat closer to the residents because of the difficulties and hardships reaching the county seat.

The next step was for the Governor to appoint three men to meet with Judge Joel Halbert who lived on the Warsaw to Buffalo trail. He lived what is now know south of what is known as Cross Timbers, at that time it was called Garden City. These men were the first law and order in the county. They were Jonas Brown of Pittsburg, Amos Lindsey East of Preston, and Napoleon Lewis of Pittsburg.

The selected group of representatives established the officers for the county until an election could be held. John S. Williams for sheriff and collector, Thomas Davis for treasurer, and Alferd H. Foster clerk of county and also clerk of court.

The name of the county was to be Hickory (in honor of the president of United States Andrew Jackson who was called Old Hickory). Hermitage was named after his home called the Hermitage, located east of Nashville, Tennessee. A wooden courthouse was built north what is now highway 54 about where the city barn and flower shop is now. It burnt down by unknown causes. Another one was built just south of what is now the square in 1852. When this one also burned all records were lost. The court was in total bumfuzzelled. The officers decided to rent space in Wheatland for a temporary courthouse the judges met in a house in the south part of Hermitage. This time there was going to be a central place in Hermitage. The square was measured off and forty by forty-two two-story brick building would be built in the center of that square. This move by the judges caused a fight between the east and west part of the county. The jail was a log building one door no windows about where the ASC and SCS building now east of square sets, this time a wind storm badly damage the court house in 1879. This happen less than a year after it was finished. The courthouse was repaired at once. A group of men was hired to build a new jail. This is the rock building in the square north and west of the courthouse. The only name I could find who the men were on the construction was JABOC BARTSHE and a fellow by the name of WENTE it was said Bartshe was a very strong and high temper man.

Stones are huge some weighing close to a ton. This was built in 1870 to 1871 the cost was $4,500. At first there were no inter cells.

Now let's go back to the courthouse quarrel. The records were moved from the temporary court house in Wheatland to the newly built court house in Hermitage this raised a ruckus although it had been voted on the site for the court house by resident in early years. Tempers flared up some of violent.

The settlement between the two sides was finally settled when Weaubleau acquired the Frisco rail road line from Clinton to Springfield.

A wooden bridge was built over the river east of Hermitage. Most people still used the ford except when the river was up. But the people still could not get to Hermitage when the river was up. The judges decided to put a bridge over the river at what is now called Clark Street. It goes on the north side of now where the school is in Hermitage. Two days after it was finished the river took the abutments out making it impossible to repair. Next the court contracted with wrought iron bridge company in 1890 to build a steel bridge next to where the east bridge is now for $5,699. The bridge that was washed out up steam was taken apart and moved to rough holler where it still serves the community. In 1869 the court contracted with a company out of Warsaw for $2,100 to build a bridge over the river south of Hermitage. This is where the bridge now sets. This would save a lot of time for people to get to Hermitage. Before this the ford was up river about two miles then to the county road that at one time was where Indian Lane is now and come into town from the west.

Roads had to be built most roads were Indian trails. Most roads were built on well-traveled paths. The road from Garden City (Cross Timbers) to Hermitage came the way mostly as U Highway now runs till before it cross Mill Creek here it turned west across Mill Creek through the Blackwell farm on through the Dickerson farm cross the ford and came out on the Warsaw to Hermitage road where Ray Tipton now lives. There was a baseball diamond on the edge of the Blackwell and Dickerson farms that was used every Sunday afternoon. The road from Warsaw to Hermitage is partly covered up at Fairfield. This road can be seen on highway 83 south of Warsaw. Coming from the north just after you cross the Pomme de Terre bridge what was once was Fairfield now all covered up.

On the river behind Ray Tipton now lives is where the first mill was located near Hermitage. In the late 1990s a fellow with a metal detector found nine fourteen pound cannon balls. It is believe in a rush to ford the river they rolled out of the back of a wagon. In the same time period a small group of Confederate soldiers were going back to their lines near Springfield carrying a wagon load of gold. When a scout returned to inform them there were a detachment of union forces in front of them. They decided to bury the gold wagon and all. Somewhere close to Buffalo they run into the union soldiers all but one of the Confederate soldiers were killed. He lived long enough to say near white crossing in a few miles.

Before this land was made a county this area was known as No Man's Land. Where the mostly unwanted people had to live. Even after it was called Hickory there were still a proportion amount of people lived because of very rugged trails. This area was off limits to any law enforcement till in latter part of 1800. Even then there were still a few outlaw gangs camped out. Most pioneers were their own law. Most of these pioneers carried a firearm with them and did not hesitate to use it. The women were mostly as good and higher percentage was feared more than men. Their attitude shoot first talks second.

PART I, OR BEFORE THE COUNTY WAS ORGANIZED

"The wants of the people being simple, their devices for the cultivation of the soil were necessarily in expensive. The wooden mould board and the sickle were almost the sum total of farming implements. As the roads were then only Indian trails, wagons were almost unthought of. Game abounded in endless profusion—panther, deer, bear, wolves, turkeys, could be seen at almost any time. The Rizer boys in 1838, killed three bears a few yards about the ford of the river, almost a stone's throw of the present location of Hermitage, and shortly afterward they shot a panther in the river bottom about a mile above Hermitage, that measured nine feet from the end of the nose to the tip of his tail.

Herds of 50 to 60 deer were to be seen quite frequently. Wild bees where so plentiful that they were sought more for the value of the wax then for the honey and in some instances when bee trees had been found, the honey was pilled on the ground and the was taken. Honey being cheaper, was used as a substitute for soap, and often for axle grease.

The Osage Indians then still held a nominal control of the country, and other tribes often passed through on their hunting excursions. The Osages left in 1837 or 1838, and the last hunting squads of Indians passed through in 1843 or 1844.

Thus were planted the early settlements of Hickory County. A people fearless, daring and possessed of a fortitude that partook more of heroism than that of mere adventure. Humane, honest, just peaceable, and generous to a fault. Their doors were ever open to shelter and their scanty store of provisions ever ready to be divided with those who had come amongst them to share with them the perils of frontier life.

They were happy and contented, and violations of law were of so insignificant a nature as scarcely to produce a ripple on their sea of quietude. But change was destined to come over the spirit of their dreams.

The year 1841 was a memorably period in the history of the territory now embraced by Hickory County, giving rise, as it did, to the terrible vendetta known as the "Slicker War", which viewed either in the light of the ends to be accomplished, or the skill and daring with which it was conducted, stands unquestionably without a parallel in the history of the early settlement of the Southwest.

Of the real cause of this trouble, the great majority of actors in the blood drama were as ignorant as the people of past and future generations.

However, the loudly proclaimed animus of their fury was to rid the county of a band of horse thieves. But as no horses had been missing, the band was more imaginary than real. Presuming that supposed causes came within the legitimate sphere of the chronicler, we will give them as they have long been and are now understood to be.

It appears that in early day two families, one known as the Hiram K. Turk family, who settled on Hogles Creek, in the northwestern portion of what is

ו as Hickory County and the other, the Andrew Jones family, settled on the place now owned by Wilson Henderson, on the Pomme de Terre
River, north of Hermitage. Not much is known of the antecedents of either,
other than what their subsequent actions would point out.

They appeared to be families of wealth and distinction in the older states.
But being possessed of restless and wandering disposition that spurned the re-
straints and conventionalities of a more advanced civilization, sought what was
then called "elbow room" in the wilds of Southwest Missouri. The Indians,
having almost disappeared, but little, other than the animating sports of the
chase, was found to interest and amuse spirits like these. Equally, or para-
mount of these, the fascination of the card table game them other opportuni-
ties to satiate their thirst for savage life. They looked at the card table as the
better way to spend either their time or money; and what began in a matter
of merriment, became serious, as one party rapidly grew richer, and the other poorer. It was the heart burnings and jealousies engendered by the losing
game at cards that ushered in that dreadful and deadly feud that for two year
hung like a funeral fall over this goodly land, blighting it with a curse, and
deterring others form becoming such, where any day their wives and children
might become widows and orphans.

The first overt act of the contending factions of Turk and Jones occurred
in this manner: the Turks' and Jones' were one day at a shooting match, and
after returning in the evening, they as usual, sat down to spend the night at
the card table. Thomas Turk pulled out a bowie knife, laid it on his side of
the table, and remarked, "this is hark form the tomb." Jones then pulled out a
pistol, laid it on his side of the table and said, "and this is doleful sound!". This
rejoinder of Jones irritated the Turks beyond measure, and from that time
they were open and avowed enemies. Shortly afterwards, there was a public
meeting of some kind held at Quincy, where the Turks and Jones again met
and renewed the quarrel, resulting in a fist fight between Hiram K. Turk and
Jones. During the progress of the fight James Turk drew a pistol declaring his
intention to use it. A bystander, on Abram Nowell, interfered and told James
Turk not to shoot, as Hiram K. Turk was abundantly able to handle Jones.
James Turk was much incensed at this interference and threw the pistol at

Nowell. For this act, James Turk was indicted by the grand jury at Warsaw, and Nowell was summoned as a witness.

Afterward, while proceeding to trial at Warsaw, Nowell in company with a neighbor named Sutley, were overtaken by James Turk. Turk, upon overtaking them, ordered Nowell to return home and not appear against him, which Nowell refused to do. A second time he made the order and a second time it was unheeded. A third time and a refusal, when Turk turned upon the witness with the avowed intention of shooting him. Nowell, being wholly unarmed, and seeing his danger, reached over and grabbed Sutley's gun and shot and killed James Turk—he being the first person who lost his life in this bloody drama.

About the time of the personal encounter between Turk and Jones at Quincy, another circumstance took place, which added fuel to the already kindled fire of personal vengeance. A man by the name of Morton in the northern portion of the county, took up a stray horse. The Turks claimed the horse, went over to the house of Morton and demanded its possession. Legal proof of ownership was demanded, which was refused by the Turks, intimating that they would take the stray without the consent of Morton. Morton got his gun and compelled them to leave without the animal. The Turks and Morton afterwards met at Rankin's (now Hickman's Mill) and the Turks took Morton a prisoner, and took him back to Tennessee, where they claimed there was a reward for him for the commission of some felony. Jones, hearing of the capture and transportation of Morton, followed, also on horseback with the intention of releasing Morton, but did not overtake them until their arrival in Tennessee. All the parties, including Morton, soon returned, from which it appears that the reward on Morton was not offered.

This act of the Turks also allied Morton with the Jones party. Shortly after the killing of James Turk, Hiram K. Turk was waylaid on the Morton road, not far from where John W. Quigg now resides, and shot, and died from the effect of the wound some five or six weeks afterward. These acts were the immediate forerunner of what is now known as the "Slicker War", so named from the peculiar mode of punishment. Deciding that someone deserved chastisement, a committee was named to capture him. The victim was then tied to a tree, usually a black jack, and "slicked", that is, whipped severely with hickory withes, and ordered to leave the country in a given time.

Articles of agreement were prepared and signed by the "Slickers" in which it was stipulated that the object was to rid the county of horse thieves. These articles were freely and openly circulated, and persons refusing to sign were called "anti-slickers", by the "slicker party" and treated as enemies.

Afterward, a religious meeting was held on Weaubleau, by Richard Owings, a Presbyterian Baptist, who in the course of his sermon, casually and no doubt unintentionally, made some remarks which the "Slicker Party" considered to be against them, and which irritated them beyond measure. Thereupon they added other articles to their former articles of agreement to the effect that in case the Baptists should rise against them, they should also be put down. This last measure caused immense excitement among the people and many allied themselves with the "Slickers".

Active operations were now begun by the "Slickers" by the organization of a company under the command of Captain Drafton with the purpose expressed in their articles of agreement.

A Mr. Meadows, a man heretofore of an irreproachable character, was tied to a tree and whipped almost to death. Other men of like good character were treated in the same manner. Meetings were held and speeches were made in which it was boldly declared that all who did not ally themselves with the 'Slickers" should be accounted horse thieves and treated accordingly.

Abram Nowell, the witness against James Turk, above mentioned, was waylaid at his own house and killed from the brush, while in the act of washing preparatory for breakfast. His widow, though raised with all the advantages of civilized life, but with a heart as bold as olden knight, after the cowardly murder of her husband and son-in-law, Dobbins, habitually carried a rifle and two pistols with the avowed determination of using it should she ever meet the cowardly assassins who had made her and her daughter widows, and her children orphans.

At one time Captain Drafton rode to her house and stated that he had been informed that her house was the hiding place for stolen property, and asked if such property was concealed there. She coolly told him that if he would wait a moment she would show him, walked to the further side of the room, got a rifle and was about to shoot, while her daughter was immediately behind her loading another gun! The Captain afterwards stated that he saw death in her eye and made a hasty retreat.

The recital of the killing of one man particularly, chills the blood. The murdered man was visiting a neighbor who was sick. Two men approached the house in the dark, fired through the door shutter, one of the balls killing him, while the other passed through the cap of an aged lady (Mrs. Bonds), cutting her ear and clipping her hair on the side of her head.

The so-called "anti-slicker", assisted by the civil authorities soon became so paralyzed that but feeble efforts were made to bring the perpetrators to justice, and such efforts were wholly ineffectual, and opposition to the "Slickers" was soon exhausted. In this dilemma an appeal was made to the government. Who sent a body of 100 militia in command of Col. Rains, with orders to kill or capture the perpetrators or compel them to flee the country. This body of troops made strong efforts and partially succeeded in restoring quiet, and put civil authorities in a better control of enforcing the law.

Some of the "Slickers" were forced to flee the country. Five were captured but were soon released either to leave or pass into an oblivion more galling than the exciting scenes of warfare, capture or trial.

But the feud, although ended as to the so-called "anti-slickers", did not cease of its deadly acts. Spirits like these could not return the sword to its scabbard and rest content. The same wild and restless nature still pervades these men, and that with a force that annihilate, they fight and kill each other. The more active participants scattered themselves from the mouth of the Pomme de Terre, Benton County, to the Dry Fork, in Polk County.

This scattering instead of quieting the "Slickers", only tended to the augment the strength of the contending fellows who still harbored in their breasts a bitter hatred of their old enemies, the so-called "Anti-Slickers". Men attended the sanctuary on the holy Sabbath Day, armed to the teeth.

At this point it is perhaps not inappropriate to speak of the subterfuges to which the active participants would resort in order to induce the more orderly to take an active part in the affair. They would visit a man, perhaps in his field, and after telling him of all the crimes of the opposite party, requested his assistance in exterminating them. Failing in this, they would, under cover of darkness, go near his place of abode, dig a grave, paste up a notice with the request that he assist them, leave the country, or take the dread alternative of a plot of ground, 3x6.

But a house divided against itself cannot stand, the parties soon lost their leaders and the followers longed for peace. Their principal leaders were either killed or fled the country, and at last peace was again had in the community.

Thus was ended on of the most unnatural, unreasonable, and unholy feuds that has ever existed in any community—with no real cause known to many of the actors, it subsisted principally upon misrepresentations, misunderstandings, and revenge for real or supposed wrongs. The active participants were for many years proscribed by the community, which proscription remained in the minds of the people until the commencement of the late War. The Tragedy of two of the principal leaders who outlived this unholy curse in which they had risked their lives will close this chapter. One fell at the head of a mob in the far off State of Mississippi or Louisiana, pierced by 7 balls; while the other, the Captain of the first County, through remorse of consciousness committed suicide in a neighboring county.

Historical Sketch of Hickory County, Missouri,
from the time of its First settlement to July 4, 1876.

In 1820 when Missouri was admitted into the union, the territory now embraced by Hickory County was a part of Washington County afterwards became successively a part of Crawford, Phelps, Greene, Polk, and Benton Counties. That portion lying north of the Congressional Township line between Township 36 and 37, belonging to, and forming a part of Benton County, while that portion lying south of that line belonged to, and formed a part of Polk County.

Hickory County was organized by an act of the General Assembly approved February 14, 1845, and named in honor of the "Hero of New Orleans", and the county seat—Hermitage—after his residence. The county seat location was a question that had at first received much attention and which elicited a great amount of contention which to this day is only slumbering. The General Assembly in 1845 appointed Henry Bartlett, James Johnson and Wm. Lemon as commissioners to locate the county seat. They met and selected the northwest quarter of section #19, township 37, range #22, in the immediate vicinity, where Early Heard now lives. They reported their proceeding to the Circuit Court at the September term, 1845, (see Circuit Court Record "A", page 3). The report was received but only partially approved as the title to the land was in dispute. Their proceedings were by the Circuit Court referred to the County Court, and the full approval thereof continued until some future time. At the September term, 1845, the claim of John Heard to the above land was obtained. The land having been purchased from the Government on the 10th day of March, preceding.

There upon the report of the Commissioner was approved by the Circuit Court, and the county seat was located at the place therein designated. The matter was again referred to the County Court. In the meantime, however, much dissatisfaction existed as to its location among the people of the County, and the same being brought to the attention of the General Assembly, it again passed an act approved December 23rd 1846, appointing Wm. Green, of Camden County, Wm. Divers of Polk County, and Chas. H. Yeater of St. Clair County, new Commissioners to locate the county seat, requiring them to locate the same within one mile of the geographical center of the county. (Laws of 1847, page 247)

These Commissioners located the county seat on the present site of Hermitage. They made their report to the Hon. Foster P. Wright, judge of the Circuit Court, who approved the title to the land designated, and the vacation, February 17th 1847, referred the matter to the county court. In pursuant to the act of December 23rd 1846, the county court on the 23rd day of February 1847, ordered an election to be held at the several voting precincts in Hickory County, on Monday, March 15, 1847, to choose between the former location on the Northwest Quarter of Section 19, Township 27, Range 22, and the location last named on the N/W quarter of the S/E quarter of Section 23, Township 37, Range 22. The election resulted in locating the county seat at Hermitage by a very small majority. The title to the land on which the county seat was located, was by warranty deed from Thomas Davis and Jane Davis, his wife, to Hickory County, dated February 8, 1847, and recorded in Deed Record "A", page 19.

The town of Hermitage was surveyed in 1847 by James Blakemore, County surveyor, and Jacob A. Romans was appointed commissioner to sell lots. They were sold at auction to the highest bidder on a credit of twelve months. The title acquired to the N/W quarter of Section 19, Township 37, Range 22, was disposed of by virtue of an enabling act of the General Assembly, approved March 6, 1849. (see Laws of 1849, page 510)

Joel B. Halbert Sr. was the first representative of Hickory County to the General Assembly of 1845-46.

The first county court was held at the house of Joel B. Halbert Sr., on North Prairie, May 5, 1845. The judges were Joel B. Halbert Sr., Chas. Brown, and Ames Lindsey. At that term of court, Alfred H. Foster was appointed Clerk, and John S. Williams Sheriff.

After making several orders, the court session at the house of John Heard, near the site of the proposed new county seat. At this term of court, James Lester was appointed assessor, and William F. Bradley, surveyor, and the different municipal townships were formed, to wit: Stark, Center, Montgomery, Green and Tyler. The next term of court was held at the house of Thomas Davis on the place where Judge Liggett now resides. The county court continued to meet at the house of Thomas Davis until the June adjourned term, 1848, at which time a new court house had been erected on the east side of the public square, where the Drug store of M.H. Moore now stands. The first term of the Circuit court was held at the house of Thomas Davis, September 8, 1845, Hon. Foster P. Wright presiding as Judge, at which term of court the sheriff, John S. Williams, returned the following panel as the first Grand Jurors of Hickory County, to wit: Robert C. Crockett, foreman, James Lindsey, Jacob Reser, Y. M. Pitts, Edward Vandiver, Geo. W. Hayes, Audley Dennis, Jesse Driskill, P. H. Andrews, Aaron Millstead, Samuel McCracken, George Chapman, Gideon Creed, John T. Thomas, John Cyrus, of whom Jas. Lindsey, Y. M. Pitts and Gideon Creed are still living in the county.

The Grand Jury were quartered under a huge oak tree during their deliberations. The first case called was that of William Donnell vs. James Blakeman, and was continued until the next term of court. The first criminal case called was the State of Missouri vs. Amos Richardson, for burglary. A nolle prosequi was entered and he was discharged. The first jury case tried was that of the State of Missouri vs. Jesse Brown, indicted for felonious assault, from which he was acquitted at the March term, 1846, of said court. The following were the jury on that trial, and therefore the first petit jury of Hickory County, to wit: John Mabury, Cyrus Newberry, Wm. R. Donnell, Jas. E. Foster, Isham B. Hastain, Abraham C. Charlton, Wm. M. Dorman, William F. Bradley, William Paxton, Jesse Miller, Joseph Blackwell, and Edward M. Callis; of whom Wm. F. Bradley is the only survivor now residing in Hickory County.

The first person sentenced to the penitentiary from Hickory County was Moses Pinkston, who was indicted for perjury at the March term 1846, of said court and sentenced September 17, 1846 for a term of two years. He was, however, reprieved by Gov. Edwards on the 28th day of September 1846 on account of the old age of the convict.

The Circuit Court continued to meet at the house of Thomas Davis until the September term of 1848, of said Court, when the new Courthouse on the east side of the public square was completed. This courthouse was in use until about the year 1860 when it was destroyed by fire. In 1859 and 1860, the present courthouse was built. The first jail was built in about the year 1847, on or near the top of the bluff in the western portion of the town. It was composed of logs—was removed in 1870 and the present jail was built in the northwest corner of the courthouse yard.

The first instrument recorded in the deed record was the reprieve of Moses Pinkston, convicted of perjury and recorded in Deed Record "A", page 1. The first deed for land was from Hugh Dowahe to Abraham C. Nowell, dated October 3rd 1842, and filed for record November 8, 1845, the recorded is Deed Record "A", page 2.

The first mortgage on real estate was from Natan Tucker to Hickory County, to secure a loan of school funds for the sum of $200, belonging to School Township #1, Congressional Township #38, Range #21, dated

December 31st 1845, and filed for record January 5th 1846, and recorded in Deed Record "A" page 3.

The town of Quincy was surveyed in 1848 and 1849, by Benjamin H. Massey, County Surveyor. Preston or Black Oak Point, was surveyed December 8th 1857, by Daniel E. Davis, deputy County Surveyor. Wheatland, was surveyed December 7th 1869, and the addition thereto, March 29, 1870, by John W. McAndrews, County Surveyor. Cross Timbers was surveyed February 22nd, 1871 and the addition thereto September 23, 1872, by Isaac R. Clark, Surveyor.

The population of Hickory County in 1850 was 2,329, distributed as follows: White males 1,130, white females 1,013, 185 slaves, and 1 free colored, with 364 dwellings and 365 families. In 1860 the population was 4,705, of which 4,502 were white and 203 slaves. In 1870 the population was 8,452 as follows: 6,362 white and 90 colored, 3,302 males, 3,150 females, 25 foreign born, and 6,202 born in the U. S., of which number 3,278 were born in Missouri.

Hickory County, like her sister counties of Missouri, suffered much from the ravage of the War of 1861. In the month of May of that year a company of men known as the State Guards was organized at Black Oak Point, in the interest of the Confederacy. John Mabary, a prominent citizen of the county, was elected Captain, Benj. F. Barnes, First Lieut., Jas. H. Gallaber, Sec. Lieut. Shortly thereafter, the Company, with other companies from adjoining counties, were organized into a battalion, of which R. I. Robertson, a merchant at Black Oak Point, was elected major. Soon thereafter, in the latter part of May of the first of June of that year, the loyal citizens becoming alarmed for their safety, those of the eastern and central part of the county, held a meeting at Pittsburg, where speeches were made by Meekin Pitts and others. Resolutions were adopted declaring their loyalty to the government of the U. S.

On the 15th day of June, 1861, they again met at the residence of Aaron Darby, about 3 miles south of Black Oak Point, and organized a company of Home Guards, under the call of Gen. Nathaniel Lyon, of the U.S. Army, of which Company, Lycurgus Lindsey was elected Captain, James Babbitt, First Lieut., and Aaron Darby, Sec. Lieut. At the same time a company of Home

Guards was also formed at Hermitage, of while Miles Dawson was elected captain.

The citizens of the western portion of the County met at McFarland's Store (now Elkton), and arranged themselves into a company of Home Guards; John P. Rogers was elected Captain, Preston Richardson, First Lieut., and Thompson Blair, Sec. Lieut. This Company afterwards was formed into a Battalion, of which Isham B. Hastain was chosen major, and John P. Rogers, Adjutant. Preston Richardson was promoted Captain in place of Rogers.

These companies of Home Guards thus organized, rendezvoused at different parts of the County under orders to arrest disloyal persons and require them to take and subscribe to the Oath of Allegiance to the U. S. and while attempting to arrest Richard Davis and Harvey Beezley, in the eastern portion of the County Davis was killed and Beezley badly wounded and left for dead, but afterward recovered. Another party of Home Guards came upon Hiram Drennon and Geo. W. Hughley at or near Cross Timbers, between the North Prairie and Fifteen Mile Prairie, killing Drennon and wounding Hughley, causing amputation of his leg.

In July of that year, the Home Guards of Polk and Hickory Counties, met at Humansville in Polk County, with a view of making an attack upon Osceola in St. Clair County, which place was then held by the Confederate State Guards, and while camped at Humansville, in order to try the nerve and discipline of the troops, the officers arranged a false alarm, when the pickets began firing and the men were ordered into line, much confusion prevailed among the raw and undisciplined troops, and many incidents, really amusing, are told of the affair. Some hid themselves in almost unheard of places. Some mounted their horses bare backed, and fled, they knew not whither, and it is said that one man threw his saddle upon his own back and tried to mount his horse by putting his foot in the stirrup.

Chapter 2

SURVIVING A HARSH NEW LAND IN THE EARLY 1800

The names we now use are from the early French trappers such as Pomme de Terre, glaice (grand glaice bridge), Weaubleau, Nianguaqa, Gravois (gravois mill), thibaut (tebo) just north of Warsaw, aux arc (change to Ozarks).

The first thing you had to be tougher than a pine knot. You had to have the want to. You also had to make the best of what you have also had to make the best you could with what you could get from the land. I do not how they managed remember they did not have.

CELLPHONE- NO PHONES AT ALL- NO CARS- NO AIRPLANES- NO PLAY STATIONS- NO TV- AND LAST OF ALL THEIR SHOPPING MALLS THEY WALKED TO. Instead of pushing a cart they carried a gun or set traps. There clothes were made of fancy furs. (The animals they kill to also feed themselves.) Their shoes now these were the latest style they could have several different colors it all depended on the animal they killed to make the leather to make the shoes. You had to plan months ahead to have the material to make what was needed, even when they needed to put up another building all they to do is step outside to the lumber yard. They even get to pick out the trees that look the best. Now most of the floors have nice soft dirt. The windows are real nice and pretty they take a deer or elk hide scrape it as thin as possible then rub it heavy with bear fat if they have it or beaver fat. They do this to let as much sun light in as possible.

Now the gas cooking range was quite different it only had one burner. It was located somewhere along the wall. It was not a gas stove but it had only one burner a fire. A large stone fireplace with made clay and grass for concrete. Across this up to date stove, you know you have to keep up with the Jones, was a rod that the cooking pot hung on that all of the food was cooked on. Now we can not be out done with the bedroom. Most houses have only one room. The bed was the wall built on short poles with small poles laying the other direction on top of this was small twigs leaves and grass. The children bed was at a rule put in the loft built the same way. Now this sounds like a very good place to sleep. If you had more than one room you were living high on the hog. HOT DOG now we have an up to date house. O I forgot about the running water and all that good plumbing the creek we hope not more than a one fourth mile from the house which water had to be carried in a bucket. To make this we go again to the lumberyard which is in our back yard. To make the bucket we get several sticks, hickory is desirable we weave them in a circle using only strips of bark to tie the sticks together with a handle made of a leather strap for handle. Now we need to set it in the water for a few days to get the wood to seal water tight. Now for that beautiful bathroom, a fancy décor that the modern wife would love to sit and watch nature unfold right in front of one of her family. NOW FIRST WE HAD TO GET A CRUDE SHOVEL OR SPADE to flush the stool we first dig a small hole with it then flush the stool by covering your hole back up. No do you think anybody would give their eye teeth for such a modern house.

The most highly prized man in a settlement was the blacksmith, with this tools and forge. (A pan about thirty inches across with a blower underneath to blow air into the coals this would make the fire hot enough he could melt iron.) He was the person that could make the community buzz. He was able to take a piece of iron and turn into steel in any shape, he could forge to pieces of steel together in a weld. From this piece of iron he made horse shoes, oxen shoes special made to fit hooves that for being very modern how many of us gets to wear special made shoes just to fit. He also made his own nails, plow beams, and also about any thing else the settlers needed. There were time he had to make a wagon wheel of different kinds of wagons if there was not a wagon maker in the area.

Back in these very modern up to date time, what was on the mind in street bench talk when they got together was how much horse power does she have or maybe they would ask how many oxen does it take to pull a load like that? The oxen was the most used animal for any kind of work (no matter what you see on the movie screen). Oxen was used mainly for working the ground, getting ready for planting, the reason they were more dependable. Most of the time they were used for going to town or visiting the neighbor. Now I think it would be a lot of fun to try to put a shoe this huge animal. These were two year old and older steers.

Each community needed a mill to get their meal ground. The Indians put the grain in a rock that they had made a small bowl shape hole in it then took a rounded flat rock and would twist the rock over the corn till it was all broke up. But the white man he was more up to the modern times so every community had at least one mill. As we have stated before there was one below Hermitage it also serve Cross Timbers. Above Hermitage about one mile a rock dam was built to store water where the mill had water power longer. The rocks are hard to be seen all though many of them have washed away after 180 years. This dam was built there because it was close to the road at the ford. Several rock dams little further up the river. First one was built ot make a swimming hole larger. For the resort that was there called Gum Springs. Now above here about a fourth of a mile were three fish trap dams about a hundred yard apart. When the river was up the fish would seek shelter in these deeper holes of water then when the river fell the fish would be trapped in these holes of water. Neighbors would bring their box wagons get in these pools and as someone would lower the water and slowly lower the water where the could catch the fish by hand. My grandpa said each family would have enough fish to supply their meat for the winter. Most of the fish were dried when they were cleaned.

Most all of the pioneers had a patch of corn. This was the important crop they raised for it provide two sources of their daily in take. It was used to make meal for several different kinds of food, corn pones, fried corn, and any they wanted in pot in the fireplace. The most important was liquid corn. The woods were full of stills. One family when they built a new house dug a large cellar under the house, hid in behind the canned goods was a little space where he put in a still and vented it through the kitchen chimney as there were always a fire in the kitchen stove. This still was never found by the revenuers. When probation came there would be a revenuers in the county. One time a revenuer left Hermitage to go to the Jorden community. No body ever heard from him again it is not known if he is still in the Jorden community now or if maybe he went on back to his office ever where it was. One thing you need to under stand at that time very few trails in this very, very rough area he might still be lost?

Another needed building was an ice house. It would be double wall with sawdust packed between the boards, no windows, and a small door. This did not happen until sawmills came to the area. In the winter they would back their wagons into the river cut a two inch or thicker chuck of ice about eighteen inches long and twelve inches wide. This would as a rule last till next winter. The ice would be placed in layers then a layer of sawdust. The story that on the river west of Pittsburg a gentleman cut a chunk of ice off and he was on it. There were quite a bit of excitement till they got him off. Back in this time the river was a lot deeper. There a hole of waster that was measure thirty-five feet deep just below Dorman Bridge. It was measured in the late 1960 at only 15 feet deep.

Very few people in Hickory County even notice they had went thru a great depression. They were so poor not to many even notice it. Just about everyone grew their own food, always had a cellar full of can food smoke house was packed full of meat, sorghum was in five or ten gallon cans the cows provided milk and cheese. We trapped or shot game in the winter for fresh meat. No you did not have any money but heck we did not have much before. Now world war two was a different kind of animal every thing was very strictly ration. The war effort needed a lot of food but to raise it a lot of the things need to produce food it was ration. It could be gotten but not without filling papers and waiting for them to be process. You never heard any complain for we all had to do the best we could. It was said miners had to endure through hardships also. The farmer produce the food the miners produce the ore and factories hum. I would bet a dollar to a donut the generation we have now would grip every day.

In the early years of the county it was ninety percent agriculture. Everyone had to raise their own food. Steel plows were very hard to come by. If you could afford it the blacksmith could take a piece of iron turn it into steel a fit it over your wooden plow beam. These wooden plow were made from a hard tree that was shaped just right, very hard to find.

Life as it was. The yearly to daily country living as recorded in several books of early pioneers in Hickory County.

A house would be built at first of logs fourteen square. This length was used because this timber was easier to handle and so most of the out buildings. After sawmills came into the community they would nail boards over the logs or build a new one. As time went on farmsteads were laid out more conveniently. A cellar would be added for a place to keep can goods from freezing. A dug well and lined with rock most of these were about twenty feet deep. Two rope pulleys were hung over the well one for water, the other to keep milk and other things cold. Next was a smoke house to smoke their meat, an out house (privy) several feet back of the house with a wood pile in between the house and privy so the wife could bring wood to the house on her return trip to the house. The house would be built with a large porch front and back. Also the house would be built where a second floor could be added as the family grew. Each house would have a large fireplace at each end of the house. Latter as cast iron stoves were introduced flue would built. Farm families rarely had a yard. Families image or personality was graded by the neatness and arrangement of their buildings and quality of animals.

Chapter 3

TOWNS OF HICKORY COUNTY

The men appointed by the governor selected the boundaries of the new county, at this suggestion it was name Hickory and the county seat was to be as close as possible in the center of the new county. Hermitage was to be name this was done in honor of our seventh president as he was called "OLD HICKORY" and his home just a little ease of Nashville, Tennessee.

This at once set off a fire storm between the east side and west side in Hickory County was not settled till the west side got the railroad. The friso was to lay tracts from Clinton to Springfield.

Every town received it name from some event or the name of a settler.

Cross Timbers first named Garden City change to Cross Timbers when a settler moved in people traded with him his name was Cross and for a new person to find they would be told Mr. Cross is by the timber on the prairie thus Garden City ceased to exist.

Preston was first named Black Jack but changed to Preston when a fellow set up a blacksmith ship that everybody really liked.

Pittsburg with a huge settlement of the Pitts thus was Pittsburg. It is to believe to be the first settlement in the area. Pittsburg is also the largest population for several years. Due to large amount of zinc, lead, barite, and a little silver. In town was growing very fast, bank several stores, blacksmith, opera house, fuel station. Gene Turner grandfather open the first hardware in town in the late 1930 or early 40. Charles friend open the first store in town.

Gene Turner great grandfather open the first store in Pittsburg. His name was Charles Friend. Ralph Nelson build the first service station. There were also a woodman club. It was a close club no body knew what they did. All of them carried an ax to any meeting. The opera house had a music show one day a week. The most popular was Slim Wilson, Jr. Hayworth, aunt Mather the Carter family (this included June Carter who went on to marry John Cash) and Bill Ring. Other bands perform, this was the band that would bring the largest crowd. Pittsburg bank did not go out of business till very early nineteen forties. As 2014 Pittsburg has close to the largest post office in the county.

Jordan settled in 1904 had an unusual history because of very, very, rough area to get into and had lots of corn processing factories. Although probation was the law a lot of white lighten was produced in these hard to reach hills. Jordan also had a mill and two stores one of which was still in business in the 1960s.

Salem, then Judy's Gap latter move a short distance north and a name change again to Quincy this part of the county under with the most dynamic change. It went from Benton County to Hickory County. It is also on the new Butterfield stage route that ran from Tipton, Missouri to San Francisco, California. The town was settled before 1843 but when the court house burned all records ere lost in Hickory in 1848 as this area was original Benton County. On January 6, 1881 the post office was established at Quincy. There were also a big boom to hit the community. A saloon, two stores, a barber shop, steam and grist mill, wooling mill for carden, and a mill to spin cloth. The first post office was in Benton County at Judy's Gap the first post office was called Salem, then a family bought the store and named it Judy's Gap then in 1850 change to Quincy (now if you're mix up I am doing my best to get it right and I am really bumfuzzel).

First known as Salem, the a family bought the store and called it Judy's Gap. The post office was established in September 23, 1840 the in 1847 to Judy's Gap then in 1850 to Quincy in the 150 years there have been 40 different post masters. The first one was Samuel Brown by 1900 the following business were listed two blacksmiths, medical doctor, mercantile store, post office, livery barn, flour mill, café, drug store, town hall, carding mill, hotel, tarven, saw mill, school house, barber shop, stage stop. This part of county was Montgomery township, named after Judge, Joseph C. Montgomery.

The school house north of Quincy was Crosslane. William Benhard gave the land the largest enrollment was right after World War II of about twenty children. Five miles to the south was Fairview later changed to Butcher by Francis Butcher in 1867. In 1886 it was located where it now sits enrollment was about 30, this land was donated by Joel Wheeler.

Sarah and A.J. Butcher donated land for the school house in 1885 in Quincy. Sometime before 1900 the enrollment was forty plus.

In 1927 a job high school was started in Quincy with the passing of a bill by the state. This bill passed in 1923 this made it possible to have a two year high school. Merton Wheeler was the first teacher there were twelve students in 1927. Later he went on to the supt. of Hermitage school, from there he became the director of industrial vocation education for the state of Missouri in Jefferson City.

SLICKER WAR

What is the slicker war? Better yet why and who before it was over most people in and around the area was involved, even if they didn't want to be. A petition was passed around you either signed it in support of the slicker war or you were listed as a horse thief. Many people moved from the area. Many who stayed were killed. The reason it was called the slicker war was the method used to punish the believe to be horse thief. A hickory limb very limber the person would be tied to a black jack tree strip to the waist and whipped with that hickory limb some were whipped so badly they died. Others were just plain shot this went on till the governor sent in on hundred troops to clear this up.

About the year 1839, there came to the Quincy area, then Benton County, one Hiram K. Turk, his wife and four sons, namely, James, Thomas J., Nathan and Robert. According to a relative who has researched the family history, Hiram Turk was born in Augusta County, Virginia between 1790 and 1800. He was in Blount County in Tennessee and then came to Missouri. Hiram had been a Colonel of Militia in Tennessee and so earned the title of Colonel.

The Turks opened a dram shop and a small store which became a gathering place in the neighborhood. Almost immediately the Turk boys got into trouble, the first account given being an assault by James on John Graham, a man of some prominence at that time.

Prior to the Turk family coming to Quincy, the four Jones brothers, namely, Andrew, Samuel, Isaac, and John, had settled on Big Pomme de Terre River, just above Breshears Prairie. The Jones brothers were known for their interest in gambling and horse racing, and apparently did not rate very high in society. In contrast, the Turks were educated and could be quite well mannered when they so desired.

At the August election held at Quincy James Turk and Andrew Jones became involved in a controversy about a bet on a horse race. A fight followed with one of the main witnesses being Abraham Clark Nowell. All the Turks were indicted and the case was to be heard at Warsaw, spring term of court in 1841.

Mr. Nowell, Julius Sutliff and Mr. Addington met a Mr. Glazebrook's blacksmith shop and began riding toward Warsaw. James Turk overtook them at a small stream. According to testimony given by Julius Sutliff, James Turk opened the conversation by threatening to settle on land which had been homesteaded by Nowell. This was an absolute "no no" in that day and time. Turk continued his threats, drew a pistol and advanced toward Nowell.

Nowell asked Mr. Sutliff for his pistol and warned Turk to stop. Turk kept advancing and Nowell shot, killing Turk. Being warned that the Turks would surely kill him, Nowell left the area, but returned and stood trial at Warsaw in April 1842, where he was acquitted. Family researchers have copies of the trial proceedings.

After the death of James Turk, the next event which added to the building animosity between the Turks and Joneses was the kidnapping of James Morton. In May of 1841 one McReynolds called on Sheriff Smith at Warsaw with copy of an indictment against Morton in Alabama. The sheriff, not deeming the papers sufficient, refused to make the arrest. McReynolds then fell in with the Turks and enlisted their aid. Morton was taken captive as he worked at a mill by Hiram Turk. Others joined them for the trip to Alabama where Morton was later tried and acquitted. He returned to Missouri. Hiram K. Turk was arrested and bound over for kidnapping Morton, who was a relative of the Jonese. Apparently a conspiracy was formed for the purpose of killing Hiram K. Turk and he was shot and badly wounded on July 17, 1841. He died August 10, 1841. Andrew Jones was tried for the murder of Turk but was acquitted. This infuriated the Turks and they took the law into their own hands. So, the "slicking" began. Hickory limbs where stripped of their bark and used to beat those whom the turks suspected of having plotted to kill their father. But as the feud grew they extended their beatings for other reasons. Finally the entire community became involved. Some of those who were beaten included Thomas Meadows, William Brookshire, Isaac Jones, Luther White, John A. Whitaker, Jabez L. Harrison. Finally the militia was called out under the direction of Col. D. C. Ballou.

Jacob S. Dobkyns was shot while at the home of Mr. Metcalf. Metcalf had been threatened by the Turks and had asked his friends to stand by. The shot intended for Metcalf struck Dobkyns instead. Dobkyns was a son-in-law of Abraham C. Nowell, being married to their daughter Betsy. Their son was born shortly after his father's death.

Still angry because Abraham Nowell had been acquitted of their brother's killing, it is believed they, the Turks, planned to kill Nowell. Consequently, on October 18, 1842, Nowell was shot as he emerged from his cabin early in the morning. Four men were seen to run away and their place of ambush was found. From that time there arose a division among the Turk gang. It is said that tom Turk was to fire the fatal bullet to kill Nowell, but he deliberately missed and Isam Hobbs was the killer. A quarrel between the two is said to have followed. Hobbs had a bad reputation in Polk County, being frequently indicted for assaults, gambling, even murder. Jeff Hobbs was waylaid and killed. Thomas Draffin was found dead, shot in the mouth. It is believed that Draffin was killed because he had sent Gladis Nowell a message that he could tell her the name of her husband's killer. In late 1843, as Tom Turk was preparing to leave for Kentucky, he was waylaid and shot by Isam Hobbs. Hobbs was arrested, broke jail and fled to Tennessee, where he was killed while resisting arrest. Nathan Turk and some of the Jones party met violent deaths in

Texas. Robert Turk and his mother returned to Kentucky. It is said that Mrs. Turk deeply deplored the violence of her husband and sons.

So ended a violent chapter in the history of Quincy, when the town was known as Judy's Gap.

We are indebted to James H. Lay and George C. Worth, for much of the information in this article was taken from their History of Benton County, which was written before 1900.

Galmey post office 1888, blacksmith, and mission Baptist. The village was first Dooly Bend then later changed to Galmey. The reason from what some old timers have said it was because of the dirt. When the soil got wet it was very hard to work. It would be silk and slimy then when it was real dry big cracks would form in the ground. This type of soil is called gumbo. The residents said it was gummed or sticky or in short gall-me then easier to pronounce Galmey. So now we have a town called Galmey.

Elkton Baptist Church, 1839, hotel, medical doctor, blacksmith, mercantile store. Where did Elkton get it's name a few of the older residents said they had always heard when settlers first came to this area large heards of elk were here so it was called Elk-Town then shorten to Elkton.

Weaubleau 1871, first called Haren. So named because of a large Indian tribe, translated in English is Weaubleau. The only town in the United States with that name. Haren was a small settlement just south of the present location after a store or trading post, a mill close to town, hotel, in 1893 John Whitker and Benjamie Wingfield open a Christian College. When it closed it was used for a elementary school for several years. In 1898 Frisco railroad from Clinton to Springfield. The town had a huge business boom the town grew to over five hundred that with the rich farming land around town. The stores were a large lumber yard, two machinery dealers, John Deere, International, bank, several stores for everything you needed or wanted, in the early 1900s a new powered mill with a rail spur laid to the mill. People come from every where for fifty years to get feed ground. The building still stands today as a reminder to what the past was.

Wheatland plotted 1869 steam floor mill, large hotel, several stores, newspaper by the name of the Mirrow. The owner sold it and moved to Hermitage.

Wheatland had three other newspapers but they did not survive. In 1894 the Hickory County bank was moved from Hermitage to Wheatland. The bank did not survive the depression. Wheatland was called Bledso received a post office in 1838 set one mile north where it now is.

When the courthouse burned the second time leaving no records of any court business from the first meeting of the judges until it all went up in flames. With a space in Wheatland empty the judges rented it for the court to do business in. they were saddle with problem what to do now. This was just temporary but some of the people wanted it to stay in Wheatland. This even started several fights and a lot more heated discussions. Bledso was the first name for a post office in 1838 it was three miles north of where Wheatland is now. The post office moved to Wheatland when it was plotted 1869.

Avery on the Hickory and Benton county line it is now known as Breshears Valley. 1859 Henry Breshears found this huge valley. How he found it is not known. Some very rough terrain hides the valley. At that time there was only one way in an it was very rough. Henry kept the valley closed till some more family could get here. It was not long till there were 500 plus Breshears in the valley. No body, and we mean no body was allowed to settle if you were not a relation. The entrance was kept under guard you could visit but not set up house keeping. Henry and Atsey had fourteen children.

The soil was rich blessed with water rich timber land and also blessed with game what more could a family in that time in age want. This is also where boone large springs is that prehistoric bones were found in latter years in a bog. Henry built a large house of large oak logs, not a nail was used all the logs were notch and pinned together. The house was two story high eight rooms. The size of the house was needed to bed a large family. After his death the house was still in very good shape. Breshear family's had several different business they had their own store, mill to ground grain, blacksmith, and in a few latter years a saw mill. The house that Henry built was sided with boards it was still the best house any where even when a road was built in the valley and a bridge put over the river on the north west edge of the valley. I can remember in the 1950s it was still full of Breshears. Breshears Valley as it is now called has a huge amount of history. In this valley is a large bog called Boone Springs that is a large are of quicksand. From this area on complete Macedon and fragments of camel, prehistoric horses, bison, musk oxen, alligator and the five inch tooth of a great cat. Under the river bluff known as Rogers Shelter. Archaeologist have dug through twenty eight feet of river deposit sediment and discovered human habitation in successive layers. Some date back ten thousand years. In 1848 Jacob Bartshe and H.C. Bulter made pumps to pump the water and quicksand from Boone Springs. When the water and sand was being pumped out the outline of a large animal was standing up right like it had just gone in for a drink of water. The molars were fifteen inches across the crown of teeth, the animal was twenty three feet tall, the tusks were thirteen feet long and twenty two inches in circumference, the skeleton was complete except for one bone. It took several weeks to get the skeleton out and it was sold to a man in St. Louis, and later it was sold to a man in London for several thousand dollars.

Hermitage 1847 Hotel, Blacksmith, several stores, Medical Doctor, Mill north of town. Hermitage went through several fires. Hermitage first school was north of what is now 54 highway. In 1887 a new two story school house was built at the present location. It was a two story building to support both the upper and lower grades. Merton Wheeler was selected as the head of the school. First newspaper in Hermitage 1869 was the Enterprise, Hickory County Mirrow was moved from Wheatland to Hermitage in 1887. In 1886 it sold the new owner called it "New Era." 1882 sold again and the new owner moved it to Stockton. A new paper was printed in Hermitage called The Index-Gazzett. In 1903 gazzett was dropped and just called The Index. In 1889 another paper Hickory County Democrat, later changed to Hickory County Republican then shortly moved to Urbana and called Dallas County Republican. Hickory County Bank was organized in 1889 in Hermitage. In 1894 it was sold and moved to Wheatland. In 1894 four people organize capital for a bank in Hermitage in 1906 it was sold to William Pitts he named it Citizen Bank of Hermitage.

Nemo 1888 trading post, blacksmith, post office and Baptist church. 1890 Hickory County population was ten thousand. People out side the county considered the residents harsh and not very civilized. But the residents did not care for they were satisfied and functional.

HICKORY COUNTY HISTORY: The Hickory County Court House in 1914. Picture submitted by Iva R. M. Herbet.

HICKORY COUNTY HISTORY: This swinging bridge served the Hermitage area for several years with a crossing over the Pomme de Terre River just south of Hermitage. Remnants of the bridge approach are still visible upstream from the exist-ing Highway 254 Bridge. It was replaced by a one-lane steel structure that was then torn down when Highway 254 was rebuilt to provide an access to the Pomme de Terre Dam.

By an act of the legislature approved on the 14th day of April, 1845, the boundary lines of the county were fixed as they now (1907) exist, except that the Northeast corner of the county was described as being at the Northeast corner of Section One (1), Township 38, Range 20, instead of the Northeast corner of Section 12 (12), same Township and Range. The act provided that three commissioners; Henry Bartlett, William Lemon and James Johnson, should meet at Judge Joel B. Halbert's residence, then located on the Warsaw and Buffalo Road, one mile south of where the town of Cross Timbers is now situated on the first Monday in May, 1845, for the purpose of organizing the county.

Prior to the date of this meeting, on April 25, 1845, John C. Edwards, Governor of the State, appointed Joel B. Halbert, President of the County Court, Jonas Brown and Amos Lindsay, associate justices... John S. Williams was appointed sheriff and collector; Thomas Davis, treasurer; and Alfred H. Foster, clerk of the county court and clerk of the circuit court, probably May 6, 1845. These officials, and the commissioners appointed by the Act of the Legislature met at the residence of Judge Halbert in May, 1845, and transacted quite a large amount of business. A great deal of the county records having been burned in the destruction of two court houses by fire, it is impossible to tell where the county court again met after May, 1845, until August, 1846, but it probably met at the residence of John Heard about half a mile North of what is now the town of Wheatland, on the 10th day of August, 1846.

On the 23rd day of December, 1846, the legislature passed an act appointing William Greene, of Camden County, William Divern, of Polk County, and Charles H. Yeater of St. Clair County, as commissioners, to locate a permanent county seat for the county to be named and known as "Hermitage". These commissioners met and selected the present town of Hermitage sometime in 1846; (could it have been 1847?), as the permanent county seat, which action of the commissioners was ratified by a majority of the people, but the good people of the west side of the county continued to advocate county seat removal until 1856.

As soon as the county seat was settled, a court house was built on the west end of Lot 2, Block 8, in Hermitage. It was a two-story frame building and was destroyed by fire in 1860, the lower room being used for a school.

A second court house was built in 1860, on the South side of the public square, south of where the present court house stands, (1907). It was destroyed by fire January 6, 1881, with important records of circuit court, county court and deed and mortgage records. The records of the probate court and the collector's book were not destroyed.

Thus from January 6, 1881, and up to 1896, the county was without a court house. Courts were held, and the offices stored away in any sort of building that could be rented in town, and county expenditures for rent were enormous. In the forty-one years between 1845 and 1896, an attempt was made to re-locate the county seat from Hermitage, to an unspecified spot, (possibly Wheatland). However, these attempts were never successful, and following the erection of the new court house in 1896, no further attempts to move the county seat are recorded.

It is uncertain as to what year it was that white people first came to what is now Hickory County, but it is likely that it was as early as 1827. The lands in this county were not surveyed and report of survey filed until in 1837, and no entrees of lands wee made until 1838. The first settlers evidently came in on the old wagon roads led out from these points as early as 1821, one from St. Louis southwest through what are now the counties of St. Louis, Franklin, Jefferson, Crawford, Phelps, Pulaski, Laclede and Webster to Springfield, and the other from Boonville south through Cooper, Pettis, Benton, Hickory and Polk to Springfield and then on to Fayetteville, Arkansas. These roads were marked and cut out, and became Government roads in 1835, under Act of Congress. The Boonville and Springfield road passed through Quincy and Elkton. (Wilson's History of Hickory County, Jan. 6, 1907, Copyright, pp. 1-4.)

There was a very early settlement Northwest of Cross Timbers, about the Benton and Hickory County line, near or on Turkey Creek, and the head of prairie hollow...

Samuel Judy, who afterwards entered the Northwest quarter of Section 21, Township 36, Range 23, (December 23, 1838) lying two and one-half miles west of Elkton... lived near Quincy or perhaps on the present site of Quincy on the "Military Road", and ran a blacksmith shop as early as 1832, and the Post Office here run by Aaron Ripetoe was no doubt the first Post Office in the county. A long time ago but not so early, there was a Post Office at the Vanrensaler Bennett place three miles north of Wheatland, named Bledsoe... Most of the early settlers came from Tennessee, Kentucky and North Carolina; some, however, came from Ohio and Virginia. (Wilson's History of Hickory County, pp. 28 & 29.)

Hickory County was organized under the act of the General Assembly of February 14, 1845, and received the familiar name given to General Andrew Jackson. Its territory was taken from the counties of Benton and Polk...

In 1861, the Union men were ordered to leave the county and in their departure a conflict occurred in Benton County, which resulted in the burning of a large portion of Warsaw. (Encyclopedia of the History of Missouri, Conrad, Vol. 3, p. 239.)

By an act of 1845 Hickory County was created, taking nearly one-half of its northern territory from Benton County. (Encyclopedia of the History of Missouri, Conrad, Vol. 1, p. 207.)

Hickory County was named in 1845 for Andrew Jackson, known as "Old Hickory", with his home called "The Hermitage", at Nashville, Tennessee. He defeated Henry Clay in 1832 in Clay's second candidacy. (Our Storehouse of Missouri Place Names, Ramsay, p. 52.)

"We have two Butterfield Stage Stops in Hickory County. One at Judy's Gap, (Quincy) and one southwest of Elkton, 2 ½ or 3 miles. A State Historical Marker marks the one at Quincy on the spot, but the other is in Elkton, but that is not authentic. It was at the Yoast Place. A few things are still there to mark the place. Two pear trees and the old cellar can be seen, also some rocks, the last time I was there." (A portion of a letter from Mrs. Nannie Jenkins, president of the Hickory County Historical Society.)

The oldest post-office in the county is Quincy—called Judy's Gap--, and the youngest is Galmey, established in 1887. In the following list, except those mentioned above the mails are kept at farm houses: Almon, Cornersville, Cross Timbers, Elkton, Galmey, Hermitage, Lone Spring, Pittsburg, Preston, Quincy, Roney, Weaubleau, and Wheatland. (State of Missouri, History of

Hickory County, Goodspeed, 1889, pp. 252-253.) (The names italicized had regular post-offices.)

ALMON (FORMERLY KNOWN AS GOOSE NECK)
This village is not laid out and platted as a town. It is tin the North East quarter of Section 14, Township 37, Range 20, on little Niangua Creek. The land on which it is situated was entered August 9, 1853. The first men who sold goods there were George C. Dunn and George W. Mabary, about 1870. A water mill was built around 1854, by either Williams or Amox Paxton. A Post Office was established in 1868, with Daniel J. Parks as Postmaster, and the name given to it was "Goose Neck." (State of Missouri, History of Hickory County, p. 50.)

AVERY
This village is situated on the line between the counties of Hickory and Benton, in Section 9, Township 38, Range 22. The first stock of goods brought there was opened by Wright & Rash, February 10, 1890. This store was opened in one room of George W. Wright's residence, about one mile East of the present site of the village. Sometime in the summer of 1889, a Post Office at the residence of John M. Breshears, was established and he was the first Postmaster. This was on the Benton County side of the county line. It was kept there about a year when George W. Wright was appointed Postmaster, and moved the office over into Benton County. About 1897, William A. Byrum built the first store building on the present (1907) site, and was appointed Postmaster, and the Post Office was again moved to Hickory County. He put in a stock of goods with John A. Jones as Manager, which later was burned. One store is all there has ever been on this site, on the Hickory County side of the line. As of 1907 there were at least two stores there (on the Benton county side of the line, as well as a blacksmith shop. (State of Missouri, History of Hickory County, pp. 50-51.)

BLACK OAK POINT

Black Oak Point, six miles east of Hermitage, was a thriving place, but was wholly destroyed during the Civil War. It now contains one store (1874).

It is now know as Preston. (State of Missouri, History of Hickory County)

BLEDSOE

In Montgomery Township. Approximately 3 miles northeast of Wheatland, and about 5 miles southeast of Quincy.

See Wheatland.

BUTCHER (ONCE KNOWN AS FAIRVIEW)

Butcher is at the west edge of the county.

A member of the Hickory County Historical Society says that Butcher was formerly known as Fairview.

CHILDERS

Childers was in the extreme northeast corner of the county, ten miles northeast of Cross Timbers, or six miles southwest of Climax Springs, (Camden Co.).

CORNERSVILLE

It was a post-office, 15 miles southwest of Hermitage.

CROSS TIMBERS (EARLIER KNOWN AS GARDEN CITY)

Cross Timbers is 6 miles north of Preston, in the northeast part of the county.

It is 8 miles northeast of Hermitage, or North Prairie, and was settled in 1870. As of 1874, it contained 2 stores, 1 steam saw and grist-mill. The population was about 150.

It is located at Section 22, Township 38 N, Range 21 W, on Highways P and 65.

The original survey of this town was made in 1871 by Isaac R. Clark, on the Southwest fourth of the Southwest quarter of Section 22, Township 38 N, Range 21 W. The forty acres was entered by James D. Donnell, July 29, 1853, but in 1871, it with other lands adjoining belonged to Elisha Kirby. About the time Mr. Kirby had town surveyed and platted he sold the farm and lands about town to Virgil S. Williams and built a residence on the town survey near where the residence of Mrs. W.H. Scruggs now (1907) stands. Mr. Kirby sold out and moved to the State of Texas about 1874. The plat of the survey of the town was recorded by the record was burned in the court house fire, January 6, 1881, and it has not been rerecorded, which makes it difficult to trace title to lots in the old survey or additions.

ELKTON

The lands on which this village stands have never been surveyed and platted as a town. The store building of Kelley and Williams is near the Northwest corner of the Northwest fourth of the Northeast quarter of Section 26, Township 36 N, Range 23 W, and all of the buildings on the West side of the road and South of that are on this forty acres. It was entered December 30, 1839, with the Northwest fourth of the Northwest quarter of Section 25, which lies East of it, by Samuel H. Arbuckles. There are also buildings on the East side of the road, all on the Northwest fourth of the Northwest quarter of the Northwest quarter of Section 25. There are also buildings on the Southwest fourth of the Southwest quarter of Section 24, which was entered by Archibald Blue, June 15, 1840, and on the Southeast quarter of Section 23, which was entered by Edward S. Whitehead, March 28, 1839.

It is in the southwest corner of the county 8 ½ miles north of Flemington, (Polk Co.).

It is located at section 23, Township 36 N, Range 23 W, on Highways J and 83.

It was named for the animal.

It is 12 miles south, southwest of Hermitage, and as of 1874, it contained one store.

GALMEY

Galmey is a trading-point, not surveyed as a town, situated near the Northeast corner of the Northwest fourth of the Northwest quarter of Section 9, Township 36 N, Range 22 W. The first business there was a blacksmith shop run by William T. Bennett, who now (1907), has a shop in Hermitage. A Post Office was established there in 1888 and Erasmus J. Kelley was the first postmaster.

It was near the center of the county, 8 miles northeast of Elkton, approximately 5 miles southwest of Hermitage.

It was located at Section 9, Township 36 N, Range 22 W, on Highways 254 and V, northwest of Pomme de Terre River.

GOOSE NECK (NOW KNOWN AS ALMON, Q.V.)

Goose Neck was a post-office about 14 miles east of Hermitage.

HARAN

Now known as Weaubleau, q.v..

HERMITAGE

Hermitage, the county seat, is situated near the center of the county, on the Pomme de Terre River, in the midst of the mining district and 45 miles from Lebanon, Laclede Co., the nearest railroad station. It was settled in 1846 or 1847, and became the county seat by vote of the people, March 15th, 1847, the title being acquired by purchase from Thomas Davis. It was incorporated but the law is not now (1874) in force. It has one school, one steam saw and grist mill, four stores and one printing office. Population (1874), about 200.

It is thought the circuit court first met in Hermitage, during the latter part of the summer of 1845. It was held in Thomas Davis' house, in the southeast part of town... The Grand Jury was impaneled, and retired for deliberation under a large tree nearby. The stump of the old tree is still there, (1889), something of a monument to the first Hickory County circuit court.

Hermitage, the county seat, was surveyed and platted in 1847, included the Northwest fourth of the Southeast fourth of Section 23, Township 37, Range 22, and is within sixty rods of the center of the county. Williamson E. Dorman (Buck) moved his groceries and liquors, and the log house in which he had kept his store at Pittsburg to what is now Hermitage, before it was surveyed as a town, but he and William Waldo were in business here shortly after the town was surveyed. The exact date when the town was surveyed is not known as the certificate made by the surveyor, who surveyed it is not dated.

The land on which it was located was entered by Thomas Davis, but was not entered until January 30, 1847. Thomas Davis, probably, settled the Southeast fourth of the Southeast quarter of Section 23, Township 37, Range 22, which corners with the town forty at the Southeast corner in 1843, or early in 1844, and built and lived in the log house now (1907) standing there, as early as 1844.

Along in those years mills were scarce and Mr. William E. Dorman, father of Williamson E. Dorman, built a mill, run by oxen tramping a treadmill, and could grind about 80 bushels of grain in a day. It stood about 40 feet South of where Albert Pitts now lives (19-07). Later he and others built a steam mill near the South fork of the Pomme de Terre about a quarter of a mile from the public square. This mill did a good business, but was about worn out at the close of the Civil War, but continued to run until about 1874. Mr. Dorman and his son, Oliver L. Dorman, and Joseph S. Hartman, built a new steam mill on Block 13, in the North part of town; this continued to run until it was superseded in 1902 by a new mill built by Eugene Belknap, of Urbana, Missouri, Which was burned June 28, 1906... The town has had many disastrous fires

It is located at Section 23, Township 37 N, Range 22 W, on Highways 54 and 254, west of U.

It was named (1847) for "The Hermitage", home of Andrew Jackson.

JORDAN

This is a trading-point started in 1904 by the building of a steam flouring mill. The main promoter being George W. Jordan of Drakeville, Iowa, who was assisted by George T. Pulliam and W.P. Clifford of Appanoosa County, Iowa. Mr. Jordan came here in 1904 and he with his associates in Iowa, formed a joint stock company with $5,000 or 50 shares of $100 each... It is situated near Stark Creek near the Southeast corner of Section 20, and the Southwest corner of Section 21, Township 38, Range 20, and about five miles directly east of Cross Timbers. At this time (1907) the mill is owned and operated by James N. Stark and George W. Huffman, and they manufacture flour, meal and chops, buy corn and wheat, cattle, hogs, and horses and are doing a prosperous business.

There are two general stores, one kept by J.J. Bradury and the other by William H. Ashley, and both are doing a nice and profitable business.

It is located at Sections 20 and 21, Township 27 N, Range 20 W, on Highway P, east of VV.

JUDY'S GAP

See Quincy

LONE SPRING

It is four and one half miles southeast of Preston, and seven miles northwest of Urbana,

It may have been located at Section 36, Township 37 N, Range 21 W. on or near Highway 65, since there seems to be a small settlement shown on the map.

MACEDONIA

It was the site of a Missionary Baptist Church, four miles north of where Wheatland now is.

NEMO

This is a trading-point and Post Office, 7 miles Southeast of Hermitage on the Hermitage and Buffalo road, at the crossing of the Warsaw and Buffalo road. A good district school house was built by the Baptist people in 1892. A blacksmith shop was built there several years ago, (date unknown). The first store was run by Thomas Bridges in 1896.

It is 6 miles south and east of Hermitage.

It is located at Sections 8 and 17, Township 36 N, Range 21 W, on Highways 65, D, and NN.

PITTSBURG

This place was no doubt named Pittsburg because a number of the Pitts family settled near it before the county was organized. It is situated on the corner of four forty acre tracts of land, to-wit: Southeast corner of Southeast fourth of the Southeast quarter of Section 25, and Northeast corner of the Northeast fourth of the Northeast quarter Section 36, Township 26, Range 22, and on the Southwest corner of the South half Lot 2, of Southwest quarter of Section 30, (S. W. 1-4 S. W. qr.) and on the Northwest corner of the North half of Lot 2, Northwest quarter of Section 21, (N. W. 1-4 N. W. qr.) Township 36, Range 21.)

The first man who sold goods there was Charles F. Friend, and he kept his store in a small log house that he built near where the East end of the Creed hotel now stands, (1907). He was there until after 1846, for he was appointed Justice of the Peace of that Township in 1846. A more substantial store building was built by John L. Hall a short distance North of Where Friend's building stood, probably as early as 1844. John L. Hall was afterwards elected Judge of the County and was later a wholesale merchant in Sedalia, MO.

Andrew J. Pitts came to the neighborhood in 1845, with the family of his father, Burrell Pitts, from the state of Mississippi, near Vicksburg. Dillard Pitts and Young Mims Pitts, sons of Jack Pitts had been there four or five years. Lewis Edwards then lived on the high hill South of Pittsburg and Charles lived in the log house mentioned and sold goods in one room of it. William

M. Dorman had made settlement and lived near a spring on what is now the Joe Davis farm a little Northwest of town. A man by the name of Veavers lived about a quarter of a mile West of Where the business part of the town now is, (1907). The first school house in the neighborhood was South of the road at the John Jump old place about a mile South of where the town now is.

Williamson E. Dorman had a small log building there in which he kept what was then a "Grocery", the principal goods kept being sugar, coffee, spices and pepper, and white whiskey. When the excitement arose about the county seat going to be located at Hermitage, in 1846, Mr. Dorman hauled his house and store and all to Hermitage, and after clearing away the post oack brush where the residence of Mrs. Nannie F. Blair now (1907) stands in Hermitage, rebuilt his house and run (sic) his Grocery store.

It is four and one-half miles southwest of Nemo and three miles north of Sentinel, (Polk Co.)

It is located at Section 23, 30, Township 36 N, Range 21 W, on Highways 64 and J.

Pittsburg is not much more than a post-office hamlet. The place received its name from the Pitts family, of whom there are numerous members in the neighborhood. It is south and a little east of Hermitage, about 7 miles, at the corner of Sections 25, 30, 31, and 36, on the range line between Ranges 21 and 22. The first settler on the spot was W. E. Dorman, and he opened a trading –place. In 1845, he picked himself up and the entire settlement and removed to Hermitage, and for some time, the place was the "deserted village

It is eight miles south of Hermitage, and contained 1 store, 1874. (It is also spelled Pittsburgh).

PRESTON (FORMERLY CALLED BLACK OAK)
Preston, formerly called Black Oak, was platted by S.C. Howard and R. I. Robinson, December 8, 1857, on the southeast corner of the northeast Section 22, and part of the southwest Section 23, Township 37, Range 21.

The town survey of this town is situated on the Southeast fourth of the Northeast quarter of Section 22, and the Southwest fourth of the Northwest quarter of Section 23, Township 37, Range 21; it is about 18 feet over five miles and one-eight of a mile East of Hermitage, the south line between Section 22 and 23. The east side was entered by Richard I. Robinson, February 20, 1855, and on the West side of the street by Joshua Owen, December 7, 1849, but Silas C. Howard and Richard I. Robinson caused the town to be surveyed and platted by Daniel E. Davis, Deputy County Surveyor, under Benjamin H. Massey. It was laid out into eight blocks, block eight being designated church lot and block 7, was not divided into lots. Blocks 7 and 8 are 211 1-3 feet square. The deed to the public streets, etc., was made January 21, 1858, and was acknowledged before Amasa Curtis, J.P. Silas C. Howard was the first man to put in a store, and he and Richard I. Robinson were in business before the town was surveyed and afterwards up to the Civil War.

Several fires occurred in Preston during and after the Civil War.

Preston is in the east central portion of the county, 7 miles east of Hermitage.

It is located at Section 23, Township 37 N, Range 21 W, on Highway 54, 65 and D.

QUINCY (FORMERLY KNOWN AS JUDY'S GAP)

The land on which this town is situated was entered by Isaac M. Cruce, October 11, 1843, but the place was settled ten years or more before that time. William Kirkpatrick entered the West half of the Northwest quarter of Section 32, Township 38, Range 23, January 6, 1843, which lies less than a quarter of a mile West of town. Gladis Nowell and Ephraim Jamison entered tracts North and Northwest of town in Section 15, December 30, 1843. The place before it was surveyed and platted went by the name of "Judy's Gap", because Samuel Judy had set up a blacksmith shop there, and operated it for several years and there was a gap or opening near this point between Hogles Creek Prairie, and twenty-five mile prairie. Mortimer Payne succeeded Judy, and about that time Aaron Ripetoe put up a country store and secured the appointment as Postmaster. He was, no doubt, the first Postmaster within what is now Hickory County... The date of the survey of the town cannot be given, because the Deed Record containing the plat and the Surveyor's certificate was burned in the Court house fire, January 6, 1881.

Quincy, 12 miles west, northwest of Hermitage was settled in 1845. It is in the midst of a good agricultural district, and near mineral deposits, and contains 1 steam carding-mill, 1 steam saw and grist-mill, 2 stores, 1 Masonic Hall, and 1 school. (1874

Quincy had been a post-office since 1867. It was platted and probably named in 1848. Probably named for President John Quincy Adams (1767-1848), who died February 23 of the year it was laid out. There are 18 other places bearing the sixth president's middle name, which was favored by his admirers to distinguish him from his father President John Adams.

It is in the northwest part of the county, 6 miles from Terry, (St. Clair Co.).

It is located at Section 22, 33, Township 38 N, Range 23 W, on Highway 83, approximately midway between Highway 54 and the Benton County line.

Quincy, Mo. - Early 1920s.
Left going back: Amrine General Store, Blacksmith Shop, Dr. Murray's office, Baldwin Grocer, "Sis" Murray's Café, Miss Rena's Post Office, and on the right, Johnny Murray's Grocery.

Quincy History

Quincy House Hotel Owned by Estes Family

RONEY

Roney was a post-office 14 miles north, northeast of Hermitage.

WEAUBLEAU (FORMERLY HARAN OR HAREN)

This town is situated on lands in Section 11, Township 36, Range 24, entered by William Hawkins October 23, 1840. It was the earliest land entry in the Township, except two, the East half of the Northeast quarter of Section 1, and the other a part of the N. M. Durnell old farm Southeast of town. These entries were made in 1838 and 1839. The first town survey was made at the instance of Rev. Emerson Barber, by Patrick Chancellor, County Surveyor, December 3, 1880, on the Northeast fourth of the Southwest quarter, Section 11, and the name given to it was "Haren or Haran". The first addition to the town was caused to be surveyed by A. A. John, August 20, 1883, by Patrick Chancellor. This survey was an addition to "Haren", and was not described as being on any forty acres, but it was said to be South of "Haren". Several additions were made from time to time, the last addition being surveyed June 2, 1904.

The Kansas City, Osceoloa, and Southern Railroad, now Frisco, came in August 13, 1898.

Weaubleau, at one time called Haran, was laid out on ten actes of the Northeast quarter of Northeast quarter of S. W. Section 11, Township 36, Range 24, and was platted by Emerson Barber (date unknown). He was postmaster, a minister of the gospel and president of the Weaubleau Institute, a make and female academy under the auspices of the Christian denomination... W. L. Snidow, for a long time the able representative of Hickory County in the Legislature, settled the place in 1856.

Weaubleau is in the Southwest part of the county, near the St. Clair Co. line, 5 miles from Collins and 6 miles from Gerster, (both in St. Clair Co.)

It is located at Section 11, 12, Township 36 N, Range 24 W, on Highways 54 and 123.

The name "Weaubleau" is of Cherokee heritage. However, the origin and significance remain unsolved.

WHEATLAND (AT ONE TIME, BLEDSOE)

In December, 1869, Frederick Kern and Joseph Naffziger, caused to be surveyed and laid off into a town, with streets, alleys, and a public square, the greater part of the Northeast fourth of the South east quarter of Sectio 24, Township 37, Range 23, exactly four and one-half miles West of Hermitage. Fred Kern built a dwelling in 1866, where the Wilson hotel now stands. (1907). Melville H. Cooper, perhaps, was about the first to build a business house, but not far from the same time. Wm. M. Dixon, Perry G. Snyder, Newman and Mendenhall, and John Sutter built business houses. Removing the prairie grass and sod, went on in a hurry, and it is difficult after a lapse of thirty seven years to remember who was first or third.

About April 1, 1894, the Hickory County Bank was moved from Hermitage, and filed banking contract April 9, 1894, and commenced business in a splendid, new two story brick building, Which stood East of the public square, where the stone store building now stands, (1907). In about a year after the removal the bank building and all the furniture were burned, but the bank vault and safe saved the bank records, papers and funds from destruction. In a short time William H. Liggett, President of the bank, built the brick building now (1907) used by the bank, and the business was moved there, where it remains.

What is now the Wheatland office was "Bledsoe", kept at Bledsoe Montgomery's house, about 3 miles north of Wheatland.

Wheatland, 5 miles west and the rival of Hermitage, is near the western part of the mining district, and is in the midst of a fine agricultural region. It was settled in 1868, incorporated in 1870 and contains 1 steam grist and saw-mill, 1 carding machine and cotton gin, 1 school, and about 4 stores. The population, (1874) was about 200.

Wheatland is 6 miles west of Hermitage, and in the West Central part of the county.

It is located at Sections 19, 24, Township 37 N, on the line between Ranges 22 & 23 W, on Highways 83 and B.

It is named for the Agricultural Product.

DOOLEY BEND NEIGHBORHOOD
It was about 5 miles southeast of Hermitage. (Wilson's History of Hickory County, p. 42)

HICKORY COUNTY HISTORY: Cross Timbers Pharmacy on the east side of the square 1920's. Pictured are Claude Clark, Dr. Clark and Hoyt Brown. Photo submitted by Hilda Bonner of Preston.

HICKORY COUNTY HISTORY: John T. Ihrig's General Store in Cross Timbers, 1920's. Also in picture is Grace Ihrig. Picture submitted by Mabel A. Chrisman.

HICKORY COUNTY HISTORY: Floyd Robertson, left and Ray Creed, right standing in front of a store on the east side of square in Wheatland in 1913.

HICKORY COUNTY HISTORY: Main Street in Wheatland in the early 1900's. Among some of the men standing in the front of the store are Bill Crates, Jim Heard, W. P. Hargiss, Leonard McCraken and Bill Harryman. Picture submitted by Elaine Payne.

HICKORY COUNTY HISTORY: Bank of Hermitage in early 1900's, located on the southwest corner of the square. The Index Newspaper was located next door, on the second floor. Picture submitted by Dean Ethridge.

HICKORY COUNTY HISTORY: Bird's eye view of Weaubleau, in 1909. Picture submitted by Mike Wood.

Chapter 4

CHURCHES OF
HICKORY COUNTY

The first known established church was believed to be the Antioch Christian Church west of Pittsburg. M. Y. Pitts was the minister. About the same time the old Baptist church west of Cross Timbers. Close behind was the Missionary Baptist Church of Elkton, 1852, dooly bend. They had three churches. Late in the 1800s, a large group of Mormons had settle in this area.

In 1840, Mins Pitts came to Pittsburg and donated land for the cemetery and the Antioch Christian Church. He came from the cane ridge camp. Meeting in Logan County, Kentucky. This revival lasted for months. He told of very, very many fell to the ground and lay there for several hours. Thousands attended this camp meeting. Ministers were Peter Cartright who became a prominent Methodist evangelist. Rev. James McGready Presbyterian minister who went on to assemble the first circuit riders from the cane ridge camp meeting. Other ministers were Barton W. Stone, Alexander Campbell, and Brother Scott. Mrs. Pitts lived to be ninety-nine years old never needed glasses not a gray hair in her cold black hair and had all but three of her teeth.

Almond in the east part of the county had a settlement built a Baptist church in 1870. Nemo Baptist Church 1870. The first Amish settlement in the state of Missouri was somewhere north of Wheatland in 1850. They were looted so bad by confederate and union soldiers, then also the roving bands of guerillas they had to leave.

Hermitage 1889, Missionary Baptist Church was built on the river road west and south of the square.

Wheatland did not have a church until 1888, then several churches. One minister I remember very much was Tom Proctor, he was five foot tall, five foot around and was as Pentecostal as they come. He preached hell fire and brimstone every night as we went, he could jump over the benches while he was preaching to the back of the church in record time. By the time he offered an alter call he had taken a bath in his own sweat. People came for miles around just to hear him. The lodge built a two story brick building behind the bank, rented out the bottom part to the Methodist and Disciples of Christ (Christian) in the late 1800s. Hermitage had a large group of church attended people. At one Sunday service in the afternoon there were twenty-six souls baptized at the bridge the end of Clark street.

In the early 1900s, Wheatland got into a church building feud one trying to outdo the other. Mr. Rogers had just came back from the oil fields where he struck it rich, he had barn and house southwest of Wheatland pledge would give twenty-five thousand dollars if the people could raise the matching funds. The members work very hard to come up with matching funds but were short. The church was finally built with a full basement a balcony it would seat one thousand people. The masons of Hermitage built a two brick building, rented the lower half and met in the upper part. This worked very well many, many years. The Methodist had services one week then the Christians would hold services the week. The Cambellists or the Disciples of Christ. Christian Church or whichever you knew them by started in Hickory County about 1906 to 1908. The largest membership was at Quincy there membership would be about one hundred in 1917 A.T. Mahaney.

Cross lane north of Quincy 1871 went by the name Antioch church. Dissolved 1876. Methodist built a building south of Quincy 1886 destroyed by a wind storm never rebuilt. Bernard Chapel- 1916 six miles north of Quincy large membership for many years finally dissolved. Fairview (butcher) church had both a school and church, church of God held services about twenty-five years. The building rented by the Methodist- Episcopal churches in 1880.

HICKORY COUNTY HISTORY: Following a tent revival in 1920 held by the Rev. A. T. Mahaney on the Wheatland square, this baptismal service was held in Little Weaubleau Creek, west of Wheatland. Pictured are Rev. Mahaney and a group of Wheatland young women, including Mae (Bradley) Lafaver. John Oesch of rural Wheatland was among a group of young men baptized at the same time.

Chapter 5

PEOPLE AND EVENTS

If I hadn't found this story in different accounts I would say: yep he had too much Jack Daniels to drink. In Breshears Valley in 1864 a large snake was seen by several different people. And one day a young lad was walking home when a huge snake rose up in front of him. It frightened him so bad he ran home in record time before he collapsed and said "huge snake". The doctor said the lad was frightened so bad his heart couldn't stand it. Later that year a group of girls walking home from school saw a huge silver colored snake laying on a rail fence. When the men when back to measure where the girls said it laid it was about twenty feet long. A few weeks after this a group of men were putting up hay when the windrows began to move, upon closer look it was a huge snake as big round as a stove pipe (eight to ten inches in diameter) silver in color twenty feet long and a huge head. Now put that in your pipe and smoke it!

One of the greatest lawyers Missouri has ever had walked into the court at Hermitage while in session trying a man for a crime. This lawyer way very good built over six feet tall with a pistol strap to his hip wearing a Prince Albert coat; with the case going bad for the fellow on trial he bolded ask the gent if he would mind if he took over the case within a very short time the verdict came back not guilty. There is no record that could be found of him ever losing a case. He later moved on the Dallas Hickory line went to Jefferson City as a legislator, giving some of the most dynamic speeches ever heard in the hall of the capital even to this day. When he retired and came back home; later was buried in the Hermitage Cemetery with a very large crowd attended. His name was Amos Smith died 1890.

The first Amish settled in Missouri was somewhere north of Wheatland. They came here in 1850. Forced to leave because when the civil war came both sides raided them. The worse was by the guerilla band that roamed the area.

Sally Rand made Hickory County and Missouri famous with her fan dance. She was raised about two miles west of Elkton. When I was just a kid Walter and Genive Herbert our neighbors moved there. One year they were going to put on new wall paper but first they thought they would tear off the old paper. In doing so they found several newspapers that had been put on to help keep the wind from coming in. the papers were loaded with stories about Sally Rand. She was a sell out at the Missouri state fair.

My grandfather would tell of going to Elkton to play cards with Pretty Boy Floyd. He had a lot of relation in the area. He had an understanding with the sheriff he would never cause any problem if he could spend one week a year there. The sheriff would always go to Jordan, no booze of any kind was allowed for that might cause trouble. Everybody would tell stories laugh a lot and just have a good time. Just being around you wouldn't know he was someone with such a terrible reputation.

In heated disagreement Jim Blackwell shot and killed a man on the square at the water pump. This happened in the late 1800s. A road that was from Warsaw to Hermitage is now covered up by the late at what was once Fairfield a part of the road can be seen just a short distance past the bridge over the Pomme de Terre arm going north on Hwy 83. Fairfield is now completely under water. The road can be picked up again at Avery to White Cloud one mile south road meanders in south direction coming past the road that goes from Cross Timbers to Hermitage on to Hermitage from here to what is now called Indian Lane then around the bluff on the Jones farm and west till it connects with is now road 190 coming out one mile south of Wheatland then south to where 254 and 83 meets then back west to Weaubleau. Remember this time in history there was no Hwy 54. This road comes into life when President Roosevelt introduced the program called WPA. 54 was built with very little machine power most of the work was done by hand. The best I remember trucks where loaded by two men with gravel for twenty five cents a load five loads a day was considered a good wage. There is a story about two men digging a culvert hole at the bottom of Brass Hill or just west of what is now road 190. When the supervisor came back to check on them the hole was way too big, his question how come you dug it so big. They looked him straight in the eye and responded because it was good digging not like that rock we been digging.

John and Sterling Jones staked the first claim west of Pomme de Terre in 1829 for 160 acres.

In the early 1800 Preston had a gang of outlaws called the Huffman gang that caused much trouble in the west part of the county. Five hundred dollars reward dead or alive. He was shot and killed by one of his own gang. Waiting in ambush one night when the two of them were to meet in a wooded area at the edge of Cross Timbers when came to certain place in the brush the shooter shot and killed him. His body was taken to Hermitage put in a box leaned up on the side of the courthouse for people to see. Hermitage had a gang that hung out on the west side of town. Nobody would go to where they had camp. One day a lot of buzzards were seen circling the air, three days later they were still there. A group got to gather to go see when they got there they found a man shot. Nobody else was found. He had a bullet hole in his head.

There is a park in Booneville and a park twelve miles south on Hwy 5 dedicated to Hanna Cole. She reported to be the first white woman to cross the Missouri river. She crossed back and forth several times had a few skirmish with Indians when crossing one time the Indians got her horses. Later she found where they were with two of her sons and she stole them back. Anna Cole is the great great grandmother of the Kellers, Hughes, and Pearsons of Hickory County.

Nathan Boone, son of Daniel Boone, homestead two miles south of intersection of 54 and north 83. It has been known as Boone Hill ever since.

Late in the civil war three confederate soldiers were killed at Gum Springs. In the 1980s Larry Wells while clearing some brush uncovered three crude tombstones they were covered back up and left alone. That piece of ground will not be disturbed again.

Just above Halbert Bridge was a small silver mine cover up by the lake. The largest mystery occurred in the middle of the 1800s when an elderly gentleman would come into Hermitage with good grade silver ore. Several people had tried to follow him but he always lost them in the very rough area of Mill Creek. Several people over the years have tried to find this mine but all they ever got was exercise.

There was a large Swedish settlement west of Hermitage all that is left is a marked denoted Swedish settlement and the side of the road the old school.

In the 1930s thru 1940s large carnival would come to Durnell Bottoms just east of Weaubleau on Little Weaubleau. The same would happen at Gum Springs at different time and a different company.

In the 1970s and in the 1980s a farmer from Hickory County won the national corn growers contest at 249.56 bu. Per acre. He also won state two years second and third several years. In total he won six years in a row.

In 1927 the year of the largest flood any of the old timers could ever remember most of the rain had come from up river. Nobody had ever seen the river come up so fast and so big. A group of kids from Dooly Bend Church came to Hermitage Revival. It was pitch dark raining lightly when they left Hermitage to go home when they got to ford at Dorman Springs the driver had just let the horses have their led for they had made this trip several times they knew where they were going. When the horses reach the river they stopped being pitch dark and not raining that much they had no reason to think the river would be very dangerous. When it was over there were seven dead. Heavy mourning was in all communities.

There was a sharp shooter that lived in edge of county close to Flemington by the name of Poe. My grandfather saw him put on a shooting exhibition at Wheatland where he would lay his hat on the ground for people to put money in while he would shoot. Grandpa said most every shot he took he did not raise his gun to his shoulder. The skill that most impressed grandpa was he would shoot in the air then as the 22 casing was being ejected from the gun he would turn around and shoot it. One time in the coal room at the Springfield police station they threw up 1,000 pieces of coal he hit 999 of them in my book that's not bad. Another sharp shooter I saw was Cecil Long he lived in

Hermitage for a few years. In deer hunting some started bragging about their shooting skills Cecil never said much until after a while he said well if you are so good ill toss an egg up and you hit that. The immediate response was no body can do that, Cecil said well I have done it a few times. Well this started the ribbing. So an egg was tossed into the air. After a busted egg fell to the ground the remark was that was luck eleven more times of just luck. Then it turned serious not a game now for this was insulting one of the guys said well if you are so good I would throw a half dollar up if I had one but all I got is a penny Cecil said that will do but do not throw it very high. Cecil gave that penny with a bulge in it to me. That stopped talking I heard out of that group the rest of the year.

In the late 1940s or early 1950s the last buggy was tied up on the square in the 1960s Watar Maberry tied a wagon and team up on the square. In the late 1960s a young black boy was put in jail for something the next day he was gone after a wide search he was found. The next thing was to find out who helped him. He kept telling them nobody of course no body believed him. He finally convinced them to put him back in the cell and he would show them. He stripped off all his clothes put them on the other side of the cell then began to wiggle his body through a very small opening. No body could believe what they had just saw. The next day the sheriff took him back to where he wanted to go and the great jail break was not discussed with all that egg on their face.

After the new jail an old black man was arrested for a hanging crime while sitting he asked for a large round rock about a foot thick two feet in diameter they found one as close to it as they could give him a hammer and a dull chisel when he was done one morning they came to give him his breakfast he was dead he had made his own tombstone. His grave can be found in the south east corner of the Hermitage Cemetery dated in the 1800s.

Sometime in 1860 or 1870 a fellow as caught stealing cattle rather than face a jury he committed suicide.

In the 1970s sheriff Taylor arrested a fellow for speeding and drunk driving. After he was put in jail they found out he was one of the King Pins of the K.C. crime syndic. They just knew there would be trouble from his pals in K.C. to break him out of this little county jail. Taylor asked Cecil Long to spend the night in the second floor of the courtroom. From the windows in the on the back or sides he could see the whole area. If and when anybody came first shoot the car to disable it; next take out who ever came. The night went very peaceful the next day on a warrant for K.C. he was taken back to K.C. It was reported Taylor came home in a very happy mood.

One year as always on a Saturday a large population of the rural community came to Wheatland to do their weekly trading most of whom traded with Tod and Peck they would bring eggs, cream, and dried rabbits. In turn they would get what few groceries they needed and also feed. Now the men did not pick out the feed. Back then the feed manufactures had figured out how to sell more of their fee. The sack were made of a nice material the women went nuts over all this they were getting for this material. They made dress shirts and anything else that was needed so the women would tell the fellow which sacks she wanted. These were one hundred pound sacks. It took three sacks to make a dress, two to make a shirt. There is a story of a farm sale of an older couple that had a sale not very long ago. The lady had a large chest of nice folded iron flower design feed sacks. They were close to the highest selling thing at the sale. Now to get back to Tod and Peck this one lady came into the cream room, I think they thought her nose was out of place by a remark she made. But we need to get back to the story, she had a five gallon can of cream and asked if she could trade that for another can of cream. Mr. Peck asked why not sell the cream no she said I need it for baking to the reply from well why did you bring it in to trade. Her answer was very soft "a rat fell into it and what people don't know won't hurt them". Mr. Peck took the can back to the cream room and after a few minutes came back with a different cream can. My father was standing there at the time this all happened. When she left Mr. Peck said well what you don't know will not hurt you, I just put her cream in a clean can.

Two elderly brothers lived by themselves west of Butcher by the name of McVey. Their toilet was a pole across the cattle manger and for cleaning they used corn cobs. One of them had a pain in his butt so he drove his self to Springfield to the hospital and checked himself in. later when he had used the bathroom, now he had never used a toilet tissue before when he did he pulled off a large dog tick. Put his clothes on and left the hospital.

One of the most widely fun events happens when a couple got married, was the chivalry all kinds of things happen, a few nights after they were married very late at night, very late, the object was to surprise them, lots of shot gun shooting or anything to make a lot of noise. This could happen even a month or so later. Now they had better have plenty of candy and cigars. I've seen teenagers get so sick from a cigar they were going to die, what did the people do well will list a few without using names. One chivalry our local doctor was along carrying a pair of hip waders, about midnight when the party was breaking up the doctor said not yet. We put those hip boots on the groom about eight inches below the straddle we tie them tight around each leg and filled them to the top with ice. Sat there another hour took them off. The only words the doctor said well he will behave tonight. Always the bed would be filled with salt if in town but the bride in a wheel borrow and the groom push her over town while the rest of the party follow making enough noise to wake the dead. One time one of my class mates got married and no cigars sometime after midnight we loaded the groom up took him about ten miles from his house in a very remote part of the county took all but his underwear off and dumped him in the river.

The Pomme de Terre dam construction started in 1957 and closed the gates in 1961. The Corps. Of Engineers mad a bad boo-boo they failed to build a bridge so the people south of nemo could go north and vice versa the air turned a bright blue and red color the only thing they could do was to open the gates our farm was under water for several weeks. We couldn't get out. My wife worked in town so my father would meet her on the other side. I would put her and our three children in the boat and away we would go the kids thought this was great. There is a water fall in the county it is in the south end of Breshears Valley about one and half mile from Boone Springs. The waterfall is about the fourteen high in limestone bluff at the head of a large ravine.

In 1540, a group of Spanish conquistadors tell of a story of a wagon axle tree. A group was returning to their fort in Arkansas when attacked by a group of Indians; they had been raiding many Indian villages had several wagon loaded with gold and silver. They follow the Osage River downstream until they came to the Pomme de Terre then turned south along the river.

Somewhere along the river they were attacked all but two were killed. They buried the loot to return to it later. After several years a group set out to get the treasure the river had changed course. Unable to find the place or the wagon. Years later people claim to have seen the wagon and wheel with a tree growing up in them, but they don't remember where. Barney Pitts (called Ole Billy Bub) had several slaves his farm was along the river, they cleaned a field and planted crop. Pomme rose and wiped the crop out. He set his slaves to build a very large bank where the river broke over into the field. Then in the spring he sent his slaves to plant to field again this time he shook his fist and shouted "now let's see you wash that crop out" two weeks later he did.

In September 1825, the area that included what we know as Hickory and a large part of southeast Missouri. A group of men formed a Wolf Hunt Company and offered a bounty of two dollars for each panther and fifty cents for each wild cat. In our area sixteen dollars was paid out in six years, only their scalps were needed for proof.

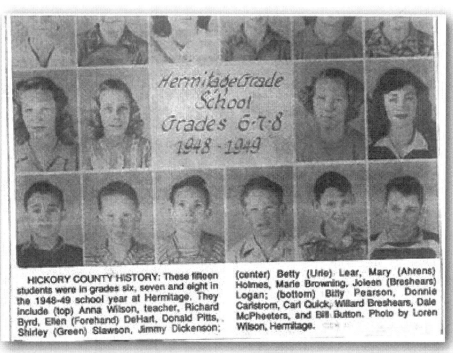

HICKORY COUNTY HISTORY: These fifteen students were in grades six, seven and eight in the 1948-49 school year at Hermitage. They include (top) Anna Wilson, teacher, Richard Byrd, Ellen (Forehand) DeHart, Donald Pitts, Shirley (Green) Slawson, Jimmy Dickenson; (center) Betty (Urie) Lear, Mary (Ahrens) Holmes, Marie Browning, Joleen (Breshears) Logan; (bottom) Billy Pearson, Donnie Carlstrom, Carl Quick, Willard Breshears, Dale McPheeters, and Bill Button. Photo by Loren Wilson, Hermitage.

HICKORY COUNTY HISTORY: Pomme de was taken on the southwest side in August, Terre Dam under construction. Aerial picture 1960.

HICKORY COUNTY HISTORY: (Left) Cecil, rope on their farm in Avery, 1955. Picture Lawrence, Lee, Sue and Elvin Kennedy making submitted by Carol Kennedy.

HICKORY COUNTY HISTORY: Hermitage School, 1930. First row, left to right: Albert Kenneth Ellison, Paul Pearson, Unidentified, William L. Pitts, Jimmy Donovan, Ardith Lee Anderson, Unidentified, Junior Chrisope, Carl Chrisope. Second row: Unidentified, John Boiler, Lewis Breshears, next three unidentified, Robert Boiler, Jacob Sanders. Third row: Unidentified, Unidentified, Geraldine Pitts-Coon, Frances Bartshe, Unidentified, Unidentified, Lucille Brown, Unidentified, Kathleen Ellison, Lucille Nevins Hunt. Fourth row: Florence Ellison-Browning (teacher), Erma Smith-Bybee, Mary Lou Wilson-Coté, Jeanne Wilkinson-Farrell, Kathleen Nevins-Liedtke, Harriet Jarrett, Lawanna Anderson-Barr, Mildred Clark-Dowler, Jewell Hinkle-Owens (teacher). Fifth row: Unidentified, Ralph Eugene Davis, Kenneth Hollingsworth, James Boyd Riley, Velma Pearson, Arthur Bartshe, Sidney Eugene Coon, Loren Eugene Wilson.

HICKORY COUNTY HISTORY: Hermitage School, November 2, 1932, Hobart Bybee, superintendent. Back row: Jewel Buckner, June Reser, Clara Diener, Wandalee Ingram, Dona Ferrell, Francis Green, Dollie Mae Wilson, Evelyna Strahan, Eula Dee Brown, Cleo Lightfoot, Elsie Pearl Stratton, Clara Wilson, Mildred Green, Geraldine Stroud, Velma (Clark) Gardiner, Gladys Chrisope, Olive M. Coon, Lucille Evans, Opal Walker, Leonard Wilson and Walter Wells; second row: Imogene Riley, Evelyn Astrom, Bonnie Clark, Johnnie Kee, William Rainier, Vincent Peterson, Leland Bales, Fred Sanders, Woodford Bybee, Lucy Pitts, Betty Maddux, Monta Belle Taylor, Mildred Crisope, Josephine Pitts, Hurt McCain, Dorothy Jarrett, Maxine Coon, Vivian Taylor, Norma Pile, Floyd Pearson, Inks Mabary, Leslie Sherman, J. C. Lea, Arlie Reynolds; third row: Fern Ferguson, Velda Miller, Ray Delne Moulder, Herschel Walker, Dimple Pile, Anna Lee Moulder, Prof. Hobart Bybee, Mrs. Mary Bybee, Mr. Merton Wheeler, Elbert Chaney, Otis Miller, Ruby Donovan, Harold Riley, Ray Sherman, Elmer Wise, Jessie Howard; front row: D. P. McGee, Roscoe Floyd, Eugene Journey, Doyle Riley, Rex Chrisope, Cletus Lightfoot, Joe Owens, George Peterson, Clinton Walker, Jessie Penny, Harvey Donovan, Clem Ferrell and Clifford Roberts. Submitted by Lucille Davis.

HICKORY COUNTY HISTORY: In a special Memorial Day ceremony in 1970, the Hermitage Lion's Club dedicated twelve flags to be displayed around the square on all national holidays. The local Boy Scout troop, sponsored by the Lions, assisted in the flag raising ceremony. Shown from left to right: Rev. Paul Coltharp, Ricky Pearson, Cliff Dickenson, Allen Harman, Mike Cherry, Gary Pearson, Bobby Harman, Joey Addington, and Steve Crocker.

Chapter 6

CIVIL WAR

HICKORY COUNTY CIVIL WAR VETERANS

The 295 names of Civil War veterans residing in Hickory County listed below were gleaned from various issues of The Index, Hickory County's newspaper. Newspaper dates are listed under "Source". In many cases, individuals were listed in multiple papers. If all information matched, only one source is cited. Where information did not match, alternative information is given (color coded as to source date).

This is clearly NOT an exhaustive list of all Hickory Countians who served in the Civil War. Two of my relatives are not listed, one who died in service and one who served for the Confederacy. Many who moved away before October 1888 are also not listed.

Surname	Given Name	Regiment	Company	Rank	Residence	Source	
Adams	Geo. N	11th Ind. Cavalry	Co. B		X Timbers	Index, 8/14/1904	age 71
Aspey	Joseph	32nd Ia. Inf.	Co. E		Galney	Index, 8/14/1904	age 67
Babb	John B.	4th Battalion E. M. M.		private	Elkton	Index, 10/25/1888	
Bears	Chas. E.	Kansas, 9th Cavalry	Co. B	corporal	Climax	Index, 10/25/1888	
Barker	E. C.	29 MO Light Artillery	Co.	private	Fairplay	Index, 10/25/1888	
Bartshe	Daniel	60th MO. E. M. M.	Co. C.	private	Hermitage	Index, 10/25/1888	
Bartshe	John	8th M.S.M.	Co. A.		Wheatland	Index, 10/6/1903	age 62
Beal	J. J.	29 MO Light Artillery	Co. M.	private	Preston	Index, 10/25/1888	
Beal	Jos. J.	2nd M.L.A.	Co. M.		Almon	Index, 10/6/1903	age 57
Beard	James	47th MO. Infantry	Co. F.	private	Climax	Index, 10/25/1888	
Beavers	J. D.	Kentucky, 15th Cav	Co. F.	private	Quincy	Index, 10/25/1888	
Bennett	Jeremiah	Indiana, 3rd Cavalry	Co. F.	private	Hermitage	Index, 10/25/1888	
Benson	Abel	8th M.S.M. Cavalry	Co. C.	private		Index, 3/1/2000	
Benson	John B.	8th M.S.M. Cavalry	Co. C.	private		Index, 3/1/2000	
Benson	McCloud	8th M.S.M. Cavalry	Co. C.	private		Index, 3/1/2000	
Bentley	J. H.	4th M.S.M. Cavalry	Co. C.	private	Hermitage	Index, 10/25/1888	
Berry	C.	8th M.S.M.	Co. L.		Hermitage	Index, 8/14/1904	age 70
Blackwell		8th M.S.M. Cavalry	Co. B.	private		Index, 3/1/2000	
Blackwell	Geo. W.	60th MO. E. M. M.	Co. C., E.	private	Hermitage	Index, 10/25/1888	age 53, 8/14/1904; age 55, 10/6/1903
Blackwell	H.	60th E.M.M.			Avery	Index, 8/14/1904	age 57
Blackwell	Samuel S.	8th M.S.M. Cavalry	Co. B.	private	Hermitage	Index, 10/25/1888	age 64, 8/14/1904; age 53, 10/6/1903
Blackwell	Samuel V.	8th M.S.M. Cavalry	Co. B.	private		Index, 3/1/2000	
Blackwell	William F.	8th M.S.M. Cavalry	Co. B.	private		Index, 3/1/2000	
Booth	W. H.	46th M. Inf.	Co. C.		Louisburg	Index, 8/14/1904	age 95
Bower (Bowers?)	Solomon	48th MO. Infantry	Co. C.	private	Urbana	Index, 10/25/1888	age 57, 8/14/1904
Bradshaw	John R.	8th M.S.M. Cavalry	Co. C.	private		Index, 3/1/2000	
Bradshaw	Wm.	5th M.S.M.	Co. H.		X Timbers	Index, 8/14/1904	age 63
Breshears	H. T.	8th M.S.M. Cavalry	Co. L., Co I	private	Wheatland	Index, 10/25/1888	Avery, age 65, 10/6/1903
Breshears	James M.	MO. Home Guards			Fairplay	Index, 10/25/1888	
Breshears	Levi R.	8th M.S.M. Cavalry	Co. L.		Wheatland	Index, 10/25/1888	
Brewster	W. R.	Illinois, 55th Infantry	Co. B.	private	Preston	Index, 10/25/1888	
Brewster	W. R.	Illinois, 127th Infantry	Co. D.		Preston	Index, 8/14/1904	age 57, 10/6/1903
Brooks	C. M.	5th Legt. E. M. M.	Co. C.	private	Wheatland	Index, 10/25/1888	
Browder	John A.	8th M.S.M. Cavalry	Co. R.	private	Preston	Index, 3/1/2000	age 76, 8/14/1904
Brown	F. K.	8th M.S.M. Cavalry	Co. C.	private		Index, 3/1/2000	
Brown	John C.	4th M.S.M. Cavalry	Co. I.	private	Crosstimbers	Index, 10/25/1888	age 63, 8/14/1904
Brown	M. N.	60th E.M.M.	Co. C.		Elkton	Index, 8/14/1904	age 74
Brown	W. S.	8th M.S.M.	Co. K.		Weaubleau	Index, 8/14/1904	age 62, age 58, 10/6/1903
Buckalew	Howard	NJ, 9th Infantry	Co. A.	private	Wheatland	Index, 10/25/1888	
Bullard	Fred H.	Mass., 34th Infantry	Co. G.	private	Preston	Index, 10/25/1888	Almon, age 58, 10/6/1903

Surname	First	Unit	Co.	Rank	Location	Index	Age
Burton	Charles M.	8th M.S.M. Cavalry	Co. C.	private		Index, 3/1/2000	
Campbell	William	8th M.S.M. Cavalry	Co. B.	private		Index, 3/1/2000	
Carlton	Tim E.	Kansas, 15th Cavalry	Co. E.	private	Hermitage	Index, 10/25/1888	
Carter	S. W.	29 MO Light Artillery	Co. B.	private	Urbana	Index, 10/25/1888	
Chancellor	Pat	21st MO. Infantry	Co. C.	private	Weaubleau	Index, 10/25/1888	age 60, 12/6/1903
Charley	Jas. H.	60th E.M.M.	Co. B		Weaubleau	Index, 8/14/1904	age 62
Charlston	Jess	43rd M. Inf.	Co. E.		Almon	Index, 10/3/1903	age 56
Charlton	W. B.	8th M.S.M.	Co. I.		Galmey	Index, 8/14/1904	age 59 age 58, 12/6/1903
Clements	Jos.	Indiana, 10th Cavalry	Co. I.	private	Urbana	Index, 10/25/1888	
Clymore	Redin	8th M.S.M. Cavalry	Co. B.	private		Index, 3/1/2000	
Collins	Wright	2nd Mo. Lt. Artillery	Co. I.		Galmey	Index, 8/14/1904	age 63
Coon	W. B.	4th M.S.M. Cavalry	Co. L.	private	Hermitage	Index, 10/25/1888	
Cooper	M. H.	15th MO. Cavalry	Co. D.	sergt	Pittsburg	Index, 10/25/1888	age 58, 8/14/1904
Cooper	W. T.	3rd M.S.M.	Co. G.		X Timbers	Index, 8/14/1904	age 58 age 55, 15/6/1903
Cossairt	James	4th M.S.M. Cavalry	Co. H., Co. K.	private	Urbana	Index, 10/25/1888	age 60, 8/14/1904 age 58, 10/6/1903
Courtney	Abram	Indiana, 13th Cavalry	Co. H.	private	Hermitage	Index, 10/25/1888	
Cox	G. W.	Kentucky, 12th Inf.	Co. A.	private	Weaubleau	Index, 10/25/1888	
Crane	Jonathan R	8th M.S.M. Cavalry	Co. C.	private	Hermitage	Index, 3/1/2000	age 62, 12/6/1903
Crawford	Henry	8th M.S.M. Cavalry	Co. C.	private		Index, 3/1/2000	
Crooks	John	Indiana, 49th Infantry	Co. I.	private	Wheatland	Index, 10/25/1888	
Cross	John B.	8th MO. Cavalry (MVC)	Co. I.	farrier	Preston	Index, 10/25/1888	age 63, 8/14/1904 age 64, 10/6/1903
Cross	R. J.	W VA, 6th Infantry	Co. D.	private	Quincy	Index, 10/25/1888	
Cross	Richard	4th Battalion E. M. M.		private	Pittsburg	Index, 10/25/1888	
Cross	William W.	8th M.S.M. Cavalry	Co. B.	private		Index, 3/1/2000	
Crutsinger	J. G.	8th M.S.M.	Co. B.		Wheatland	Index, 8/14/1904	age 66
Daniels	B. L.	11th MO. Cavalry	Co. H., K.	private	Crosstimbers	Index, 10/25/1888	age 65, 8/14/1904
Daugherty	J. N.	8th M.S.M. Cavalry	Co. L.	private	Climax	Index, 10/25/1888	
Daugherty	W. P.	Kansas, 1st mtd inf	Co. D.	private	Wheatland	Index, 10/25/1888	age 62, 8/14/1904
Davis	D. S.	31st MO. Infantry	Co. F.	private	Urbana	Index, 10/25/1888	
Davis	Wm. J.	31st MO. Infantry	Co. F.	private	Lone Spring	Index, 10/25/1888	
Delmont	Lewis	8th M.S.M. Cavalry	Co. C.	private		Index, 3/1/2000	
Delozier	Joseph	60th MO. E. M. M.	Co. K.	private	Quincy	Index, 10/25/1888	
Dent	E.	60th MO. E. M. M.	Co.	private	Wheatland	Index, 10/25/1888	
Dent	Samuel	8th M.S.M. Cavalry	Co. C.	private		Index, 3/1/2000	
Dent	Samuel, sr.	8th M.S.M. Cavalry	Co. A.	private	Wheatland	Index, 10/25/1888	
Dixon	William M.	8th M.S.M. Cavalry	Co. C.	private		Index, 3/1/2000	
Dobbs	Wm.	Home Guards			Hermitage	Index, 8/14/1904	age 60
Dollarhide	J. C.	State Guard			Hermitage	Index, 8/14/1904	age 80
Dollarhide	Jesse	8th M.S.M. Cavalry	Co. B.	private		Index, 3/1/2000	
Dorley	Daniel	184th Ohio Inf.	Co. C.		Wheatland	Index, 10/8/1903	age 60
Donovan	W. R.	30th Ky. Mt. Inf.	Co. G.		Galmey	Index, 8/14/1904	age 63
Dooley	John	8th M.S.M. Cavalry	Co. C.	private		Index, 3/1/2000	
Dooley	William H.	8th M.S.M. Cavalry	Co. C.	private		Index, 3/1/2000	
Dooley	Wm. H.	8th M.S.M. Cavalry	Co. B.	private	Conway	Index, 10/25/1888	
Dorman	Michael W.	8th M.S.M. Cavalry	Co. C.	private	Pittsburg	Index, 10/25/1888	
East	Thomson	24th Iowa Inf.	Co. K.		Wheatland	Index, 10/8/1903	age 78
Eddie	John	60th E.M.M.	—		Preston	Index, 8/14/1904	age 73
Edwards	Wm.	Ohio, 32nd Infantry	Co. F.	private	Fairplay	Index, 10/25/1888	
Ellerman [Ellman]	J. C.	22nd Ind. Inf.	—		Hermitage	Index, 8/14/1904	age 58 age 59, 10/6/1903
Ellison	Charles	8th M.S.M. Cavalry	Co. B.	private		Index, 3/1/2000	
Eskew	D. P.	23rd MO. Infantry	Co. K.	private	Urbana	Index, 10/25/1888	age 58, 8/14/1904
Evans	John A.	8th M.S.M. Cavalry	Co. B.	private		Index, 3/1/2000	
Fidler	Jas.	Kansas, 15th Cavalry	Co. B.	private	Climax	Index, 10/25/1888	
Floyd	D. B.	36th E.M.M.	Co. G.		Elkton	Index, 10/8/1903	age 73
Fortune	Richard	Kansas, 10th Cavalry	Co. I.	private	Montevallo	Index, 10/25/1888	

Foster	J. W.	32nd N.C. Inf.	Co. I		Hermitage	Index, 8/14/1904	age 71
Freeman	Lewis	8th M.S.M. Cavalry	Co. B	private	Wheatland	Index, 10/25/1888	
Fugate	Ben. F.	8th M.S.M. Cavalry	Co. L	private	Urbana	Index, 10/25/1888	
Gardner	Geo. W.	60th MO. E. M. M.	Co. C	private	Wheatland	Index, 10/25/1888	
Gardner	James M.	60th MO. E. M. M.	Co. C	private	Wheatland	Index, 10/25/1888	age 70, 8/14/1904
Gasway	Saml	U.S., det 14th inf		private	Hermitage	Index, 10/25/1888	
Glassbrook	R. W.	Arkansas, 1st Cavalry	Co. B	private	Wheatland	Index, 10/25/1888	
Graves	George W.	8th M.S.M. Cavalry	Co. B	private		Index, 3/1/2000	
Graves	J. W.	3rd Ind. Cav	Co. B		Douglas, Ks.	Index, 10/5/1903	age 83
Hackney	J. F.	4th M.V.C. (7th MVC)	Co. D		Hermitage	Index, 8/14/1904	age 70, age 58, 10/25/1903
Halbert	Ephraim F.	8th M.S.M. Cavalry	Co. B	private	Hermitage	Index, 10/25/1888	age 72, 8/14/1904
Halbert	Joel B.	8th M.S.M. Cavalry	Co. B	private	X Timbers	Index, 3/1/2000	age 64, 8/14/1904
Halbert	William	11th MO. Cavalry	Co. H	private	Pittsburg	Index, 10/25/1888	
Hall	D. W.	MO. Home Guards			Preston	Index, 10/25/1888	
Harden	Reuben	26th MO. Infantry	Co. I	sergt	Quincy	Index, 10/25/1888	
Hart	George A.	8th M.S.M. Cavalry	Co. B	private		Index, 3/1/2000	
Hart	John M.	8th M.S.M. Cavalry	Co. B	private	X Timbers	Index, 3/1/2000	age 61, 8/14/1904
Hartley	Jesse	8th M.S.M. Cavalry	Co. C	private	Weaubleau	Index, 3/1/2000	age 61, 8/14/1904
Heard	Early	60th E.M.M.	Co. C		Wheatland	Index, 8/14/1904	age 69
Heard	John	8th MO. Cavalry	Co. M	private	Wheatland	Index, 10/25/1888	
Henry	Wm.	Indiana, 89th Infantry	Co. E	private	Climax	Index, 10/25/1888	
Hewitt	John S.	Ohio, 116th Infantry	Co. G	private	Wheatland	Index, 10/25/1888	age 72, 8/14/1904
Hiatt	W. W.	Indiana, 11th Infantry	Co. F	1st lieut	Hermitage	Index, 10/25/1888	
Hickman	William C.	8th M.S.M. Cavalry	Co. B	private	X Timbers	Index, 3/1/2000	age 62, 8/14/1904
Hinkle	Gideon	8th M.S.M. Cavalry	Co. C	bugler	Louisburg	Index, 10/25/1888	
Hobbs	Newberry	8th M.S.M. Cavalry	Co. B	private		Index, 3/1/2000	
Hodgen	A.	Arkansas, 1st Cavalry	Co. C	private	Crosstimbers	Index, 10/25/1888	
Hogg	John	8th M.S.M. Cavalry	Co. C	private		Index, 3/1/2000	
Hogg	William	8th M.S.M. Cavalry	Co. C	private		Index, 3/1/2000	
Hollingsworth	A.	38th Ind. Inf.	Co. E	private	Galmey	Index, 10/25/1888	age 75, 8/14/1904
Holt	H. M.	60th MO. E. M. M.	Co. H	private	Preston	Index, 10/25/1888	
Holt	H. M.	1st Prol. E.M.M.	Co. B		Preston	Index, 8/14/1904	age 56
House	Andrew J.	8th M.S.M. Cavalry	Co. C	private	Pittsburg	Index, 10/25/1888	
Jackson	John	60th MO. E. M. M.	Co. C	private	Preston	Index, 10/25/1888	
James	W. B.	1st MO Light Artillery	Co. E	private	Urbana	Index, 10/25/1888	
Jamison	Harrison H.	8th M.S.M. Cavalry	Co. C	private		Index, 3/1/2000	
Johnson	James G.	1st M.S.M. Cavalry	Co. G	private	Hermitage	Index, 10/25/1888	
Johnson	Wm. C.	8th M.S.M. Cavalry	Co. B	private	Pittsburg	Index, 10/25/1888	
Jones	John H.	8th M.S.M. Cavalry	Co. C	private		Index, 3/1/2000	
Jones	W. A.	1st Ark Cavalry	Co. C		Almon	Index, 8/14/1904	age 63
Jordan	Alexander C.	8th M.S.M. Cavalry	Co. B	private		Index, 3/1/2000	
Jordan	Jasper N.	8th M.S.M. Cavalry	Co. A	private	Hermitage	Index, 10/25/1888	
Jordan	John W.	8th M.S.M. Cavalry	Co. B	private		Index, 3/1/2000	
Jordan	Wm. N.	8th M.S.M. Cavalry	Co. I	private	Hermitage	Index, 10/25/1888	age 74, 8/14/1904
Jordan	Wm. R.	60th MO. E. M. M.	Co. C	private	Wheatland	Index, 10/25/1888	
Jordan	Wm. T.	8th M.S.M. Cavalry	Co. B	private	Hermitage	Index, 10/25/1888	age 64, XTimbers, 8/14
Karnes	W. A.	Ohio, 38th Infantry	Co. A	private	Pleasant Hope	Index, 10/25/1888	
Kelley	G. C.	2nd Ia Inf	Co. H		Wheatland	Index, 8/14/1904	age 63
Kendle	E.	Illinois, 6th Infantry	Co. G	private	Preston	Index, 10/25/1888	
Knight	Joseph	8th M.S.M. Cavalry	Co. B	private	Preston	Index, 10/25/1888	
Kroff	Chas.	Indiana, 11th Infantry	Co. F	2d lieut	Hermitage	Index, 10/25/1888	
Lair	D. L.	Illinois, 2nd Light Art.	Co. A	private	Wheatland	Index, 10/25/1888	
Lankford	William R.	8th M.S.M. Cavalry	Co. C	private		Index, 3/1/2000	
Larose	Aaron	4th Battalion E. M. M.		private	Pittsburg	Index, 10/25/1888	
Lewis	John	8th M.S.M. Cavalry	Co. C	private	Preston	Index, 10/25/1888	
Lewis	Richard	4th Battalion E. M. M.		private	Preston	Index, 10/25/1888	
Lewis	Richard	60th E.M.M. - 1st E.M.M.	Co. C		Preston	Index, 8/14/1904	age 58
Liggett	William H.	8th M.S.M. Cavalry	Co. B	private		Index, 3/1/2000	

Surname	Name	Unit	Co.	Rank	Place	Index	Notes
Liggett	Wm. H.	8th M.S.M. Cavalry	Co. L.	sergt major of bat	Wheatland	Index, 10/25/1888	
Lindsey	Alfred	8th M.S.M. Cavalry	Co. B	private	Preston	Index, 10/25/1888	
Lindsey	Jno. J.	8th M.S.M. Cavalry	Co. B	private	Preston	Index, 10/25/1888	age 70, 8/14/1904
Lindsey	John	8th M.S.M. Cavalry	Co. B	Captain		Index, 3/1/2000	
Lindsey	Lycurgus	8th M.S.M. Cavalry	Co. B	lieutenant	Lone Spring	Index, 10/25/1888	age 78, 8/14/1904
Lindsey	Thos.	8th M.S.M. Cavalry	Co. B	private	Lone Spring	Index, 10/25/1888	
Lopp	John	8th M.S.M. Cavalry	Co. C.	private		Index, 3/1/2000	
Lopp	Samuel	8th M.S.M. Cavalry	Co. C.	private		Index, 3/1/2000	
Lord	Thos. H.	8th M.S.M. Cavalry	Co. L.	private	Hermitage	Index, 10/25/1888	
Lord	Wm. H.	8th M.S.M. Cavalry	Co. L.	private	Weaubleau	Index, 10/25/1888	
Mabary	G. W.	9th M.S.M.	Co. K.		Preston	Index, 8/14/1904	age 63
Mabary	W. J.	9th M.S.M.	Co. K.		Preston	Index, 10/3/1903	age 67
Martin	Timothy	19th MO. Cavalry	Co. D.	private	Weaubleau	Index, 10/25/1888	
Mashburn	B. F.	14th MO. Cavalry	Co. H.	private	Hermitage	Index, 10/25/1888	
Mashburn	George W.	8th M.S.M. Cavalry	Co. C.	private	Elkton	Index, 3/1/2000	age 58, 10/9/1903
Mashburn	H. C.	14th M.V.C.	Co. I.		Galmey	Index, 10/9/1903	age 55
Mashburn	James H.	8th M.S.M. Cavalry	Co. C.	private		Index, 3/1/2000	
Mashburn	M. C.	14th MO. Cavalry	Co. I.	private	Hermitage	Index, 10/25/1888	
Mashburn	Wm.	60th E.M.M.	Co. C.		Elkton	Index, 10/9/1903	age 74
Mathews	J. N.	8th M.S.M.	Co. K.		Almon	Index, 10/9/1903	age 67
Mawhinney	William A.	8th M.S.M. Cavalry	Co. B	private		Index, 3/1/2000	
McAfee	Henry	8th M.S.M. Cavalry	Co. B	private		Index, 3/1/2000	
McAfee	M. C.	8th M.S.M. Cavalry	Co. B	private		Index, 3/1/2000	
McCaslin	W. L.	60th E.M.M.	Co. C.	lieut.	Wheatland	Index, 10/25/1888	age 62, 8/14/1904
McClure	John B.	13th MO. Cavalry	Co.	private	Hermitage	Index, 10/25/1888	
McCracken	Wm.	8th M.S.M. Cavalry	Co. C.	private	Hermitage	Index, 10/25/1888	Hammerville, age55, 3/2
McKenzie	G. W.	Illinois, 11th Infantry	Co. G.	private	Hermitage	Index, 10/25/1888	
Miller	Thad W.	8th M.S.M. Cavalry	Co. C.	private		Index, 3/1/2000	
Mitchener	T. J.	8th M.S.M.	Co. B		X Timbers	Index, 10/9/1903	age 60
Monroe	Jno. P.	2nd Kan. Lt. Art.			Weaubleau	Index, 10/9/1903	age 66
Montgomery	J. J.	11th Mo. Inf.	Co. D.		Hermitage	Index, 8/14/1904	age 78
Moore	Jesse F. D.	8th M.S.M. Cavalry	Co. B	private	Crosstimbers	Index, 10/25/1888	
Moore	William H.	8th M.S.M. Cavalry	Co. B	private		Index, 3/1/2000	
Moore	Wm. G.	8th M.S.M. Cavalry	Co. C	private	Wheatland	Index, 10/25/1888	
Moore	Wm. G.	60th MO. E.M.M.	Co.	private	Preston	Index, 10/25/1888	
Morgan	A.	8th M.S.M.	Co. B		Preston	Index, 8/14/1904	age 67
Morgan	A.	MO. Home Guards			Preston	Index, 10/25/1888	
Morgan	Ach'g.	Hickory Co. Home Guards	Co. D.		Preston	Index, 10/9/1903	age 56
Morton	J. A.	8th M.S.M.	Co. I.		Wheatland	Index, 8/14/1904	age 74
Murphy	Geo. W.	8th M.S.M. Cavalry	Co. L.	private	Wheatland	Index, 10/25/1888	
Mustain	T. E.	14th M.V.C.	Co. D.		Almon	Index, 8/14/1904	age 60
Neale	J. H.	Indiana, 154th Infantry	Co. I.	private	Crosstimbers	Index, 10/25/1888	
Neihardt	M. N.	Ohio, 88th Infantry	Co. E.	private	Hermitage	Index, 10/25/1888	age 57, 8/14/1904
Nelson	J. C.	15th MO. Cavalry	Co. B.	private	Urbana	Index, 10/25/1888	
Nix	Stephen	37th Ky. Inf.	Co. F.		X Timbers	Index, 8/14/1904	age 64
Nunn	Jas. H.	7th Pro. E.M.M.	Co. D.		Weaubleau	Index, 8/14/1904	age 66
Nutter	E. D.	2nd Ohio Lt. Artillery	Co. G.		Hermitage	Index, 8/14/1904	age 63
Pack	J. R.	MO. Home Guards		surgeon	Hermitage	Index, 10/25/1888	
Patterson	John C.	Iowa, 3rd Cavalry	Co. E	private	Urbana	Index, 10/25/1888	
Paxton	John W.	60th MO. E.M.M.	Co. B.	private	Wheatland	Index, 10/25/1888	
Perry	S. P.	122nd Ill. Inf.	Co. B.		Weaubleau	Index, 10/9/1903	age 72
Pliant?	T. J.	Kentucky, 2th Inf?	Co. D.	private	Wheatland	Index, 10/25/1888	
Pitts	A. J.	47th E.M.M.	Co. H.		Hermitage	Index, 8/14/1904	age 74
Pitts	Ben	46th MO. Infantry	Co. B.	private	Pittsburg	Index, 10/25/1888	
Pitts	C. C.	8th M.S.M.	Co. A.		Galmey	Index, 8/14/1904	age 64, age 62, 10/9/1903
Pitts	Frances M.	8th M.S.M. Cavalry	Co. C.	private		Index, 3/1/2000	
Pitts	James Ewell	8th M.S.M. Cavalry	Co. C.	private		Index, 3/1/2000	
Pitts	James M.	8th M.S.M. Cavalry	Co. C.	private		Index, 3/1/2000	

Pitts	John B.	8th M.S.M. Cavalry	Co. C.	private		Index, 3/1/2000	
Pitts	Jonathan T.	8th M.S.M. Cavalry	Co. C.	private		Index, 3/1/2000	
Pitts	Logan T.	8th M.S.M. Cavalry	Co. C.	private		Index, 3/1/2000	
Pitts	M. M.	8th M.S.M. Cavalry	Co. C.	private		Index, 3/1/2000	
Pitts	William C.	8th M.S.M. Cavalry	Co. C.	private		Index, 3/1/2000	
Pitts	William D.	8th M.S.M. Cavalry	Co. C.	private		Index, 3/1/2000	
Pitts	William N.	8th M.S.M. Cavalry	Co. C.	private	Pittsburg	Index, 3/1/2000	age 61, 8/14/1904 age 61, 10/8/1903
Pope	N. K.	8th M.V.C.	Co. M.		Preston	Index, 8/14/1904	age 61
Quick	Jesse	6th M.S.M.	Co. K.		X Timbers	Index, 8/14/1904	age 62
Rains	James M.	8th M.S.M. Cavalry	Co. B.	private		Index, 3/1/2000	
Rains	William R.	8th M.S.M. Cavalry	Co. B.	2nd lieutenant		Index, 3/1/2000	
Ramsey	J. A.	18th Ia Inf.	Co. D		Urbana	Index, 8/14/1904	age 65
Ramsey	James H.	48th MO. Infantry	Co. A.	private	Quincy	Index, 10/25/1888	
Raymond	James H.	6th M.S.M. Cavalry	Co. L.	sergt	Quincy	Index, 10/25/1888	
Redder	A. B.	Hick Co. H. G.	Co. D.		Pittsburg	Index, 8/14/1904	age 74
Reser	L. N.	8th MO. Cavalry	Co. I.	private	Urbana	Index, 10/25/1888	
Reser	W. F.	14th M.V.C.	Co. H.		Preston	Index, 10/8/1903	age 53
Revel	J. H.	2nd M.S.M.	Co. I.		Savannah	Index, 8/14/1904	age 69
Rhea	B. T.	6th M.S.M. Cavalry	Co. B.	private		Index, 3/1/2000	
Richards	Leonard	8th M.S.M. Cavalry	Co. C.	2nd lieutenant		Index, 3/1/2000	
Richards	Meredith	8th M.S.M. Cavalry	Co. C.	private		Index, 3/1/2000	
Riddle	Joseph	14th MO. Cavalry	Co. H.	private	Preston	Index, 10/25/1888	age 37, 8/14/1904
Robbins	P. E.	1. P.E.M.M.	Co. B.		Preston	Index, 10/8/1903	age 67
Robertson	J. A.	6th M.V.C.	Co. D.		Preston	Index, 8/14/1904	age 79
Robertson	James A.	8th M.S.M. Cavalry	Co. B.	private	Preston	Index, 10/25/1888	age 64, 8/14/1904
Robertson	William A.	8th M.S.M. Cavalry	Co. B.	private		Index, 3/1/2000	
Roney	Geo. H.	Hickory Co. Home Guards	Co. A.		X Timbers	Index, 10/8/1903	age 59
Rountree	William R.	8th M.S.M. Cavalry	Co. C.	private		Index, 3/1/2000	
Sanders	J. A.	4th M.S.M. Cavalry	Co. B.	private	Hermitage	Index, 10/25/1888	
Sanders	J. H.	4th M.S.M.	Co. B. M.		Hermitage	Index, 8/14/1904	age 73
Sanders	W. W.	4th M.S.M. Cavalry	Co. B.	private	Hermitage	Index, 10/25/1888	age 63, 8/14/1904
Scott	E. F.	5th Ind. Cav.	Co. H.		Almon	Index, 10/8/1903	age 61
Scott	E. W.	71st Ill. Inf.	Co. I.		Wheatland	Index, 8/14/1904	age 65
Selby	S. B.	47th Ir E.M.M.	Co. H.		Preston	Index, 8/14/1904	age 65
Shinn	Wm. J.	6th W Va Inf.	Co. E.		Hermitage	Index, 10/8/1903	age 71
Shull	Henry	8th M.S.M. Cavalry	Co. F.	private	Crosstimbers	Index, 10/25/1888	
Shumate	Martin	7th M.S.M.	Co. G.		Preston	Index, 10/25/1888	age 67
Simmons	B. F.	2nd MO. Light Artillery	Co. I.	private	Preston	Index, 10/25/1888	age 61, 8/14/1904
Simmons	Joel Y.	47th MO. Infantry	Co. C.	private	Climax	Index, 10/25/1888	
Simpson	Nathaniel	8th M.S.M. Cavalry	Co. B.	private		Index, 3/1/2000	
Skinner	R. D.	Kansas, 1st Cavalry	Co. B.	private	Wheatland	Index, 10/25/1888	
Skinner	Thomas T.	8th M.S.M. Cavalry	Co. B.	private		Index, 3/1/2000	
Skinner	William	8th M.S.M. Cavalry	Co. B.	private		Index, 3/1/2000	
Smith	A. J.	24th Mo. Inf.	Co. C.		Galmey	Index, 10/8/1903	age 63
Smith	Geo.	Iowa, 2d Infantry	Co. F.	private	Crosstimbers	Index, 10/25/1888	
Smith	Isaac C.	12th MO. Cavalry	Co. I.	private	Hermitage	Index, 10/25/1888	8/14/1904; age 63, Wife
Smith	Michael	Kansas, 2d Cavalry	Co. L.	private		Index, 10/25/1888	
Southerly	E. S.	11th Michigan Inf.	Co. E.		Hermitage	Index, 10/8/1903	age 75
Spencer	Chas.	8th M.V.C.	Co. M.		X Timbers	Index, 8/14/1904	age 62
Stanley	John	8th M.S.M.	Co. B.		Violet	Index, 8/14/1904	age 57
Starkey	Bennett	8th M.S.M. Cavalry	Co. C.	private		Index, 3/1/2000	
Stephenson	T.	25th Ohio Vol Cav.	Co. I.		Preston	Index, 8/14/1904	age 65
Stitz	Lyman W.	8th M.S.M. Cavalry	Co. B.	1st sergeant		Index, 3/1/2000	
Stout	John W.	6th M.S.M.	Co. D.		Pittsburg	Index, 8/14/1904	age 59
Stroud	Jesse	Arkansas, 2nd Cavalry	Co. K.	private	Hermitage	Index, 10/25/1888	
Stull	John	6th W Va Inf.	Co. C.		Avery	Index, 8/14/1904	age 58
Sutz	C. C.	Indiana, 51st Infantry	Co. E.	private	Wheatland	Index, 10/25/1888	

Suit	Jas. W.	Indiana, 42nd Infantry	Co. E	private	Wheatland	Index, 10/25/1888	
Taylor	D. P.	78th Ill. Inf.	Co. G		X Timbers	Index, 8/1/1904	age 63
Taylor	E. N.	Tenn. 8th Infantry	Co. A	private	Hermitage	Index, 10/25/1888	age 56, 8/14/1904
Tharp	C. C.	4th M.S.M. Cavalry	Co. M	private	Urbana	Index, 10/25/1888	
Tillery	Andrew J.	8th M.S.M. Cavalry	Co. C	private		Index, 3/1/2000	
Tracy	John P.	8th M.S.M.	Co. A, D		Springfield	Index, 8/14/1904	age 68
Tucker	N. R.	46th MO. Infantry	Co. L	private	Lone Spring	Index, 10/25/1888	
Turner	D. F.	7th MO. Cavalry	Co. M	private	Urbana	Index, 10/25/1888	
Turner	W. H.	2nd Conn. H.A.	Co. E		Lebanon	Index, 8/14/1904	age 59
Vance	R. A.	Indiana, 72d Infantry	Co. I	captain	Hermitage	Index, 10/25/1888	
Vogel	John	5th MO. Cavalry	Co. E	private	Climax	Index, 10/25/1888	
Walker	Wm. C	12th M.V.C.	Co. D	private	Urbana	Index, 10/25/1888	age 56
Wallen	James F.	8th M.S.M. Cavalry	Co. L	private	Wheatland	Index, 10/25/1888	
Wammes?	S. A.	23rd M.S.M. Cavalry	Co. G	private	Preston	Index, 10/25/1888	
Whelchel	Charles M. Jr.	8th M.S.M. Cavalry	Co. B	private		Index, 3/1/2000	
Whelchel	Charles M. Sr.	8th M.S.M. Cavalry	Co. B	private		Index, 3/1/2000	
Whitaker	J	1st Ind. H.A.	Co. D		Weaubleau	Index, 8/14/1904	age 61
Williams	Nathaniel P.	8th M.S.M. Cavalry	Co. B	private	Wheatland	Index, 10/25/1888	age 63, 8/14/1904
Wilson	David	8th MO. Cavalry	Co. H	private	Crosstimbers	Index, 10/25/1888	
Wilson	Geo.	10th MO. Cavalry	Co. B	private	Hermitage	Index, 10/25/1888	
Wilson	James R.	Pro. E.M.M.			Quincy	Index, 8/14/1904	age 58
Wilson	L. L.	North Carolina, 3rd Mtd Inf	Co. F	private	Weaubleau	Index, 10/25/1888	
Wilson	Pleasant	10th MO. Cavalry	Co. B	private	Preston	Index, 10/25/1888	age 63, 8/14/1904
Wilson	Wm	1st Ky. Inf	Co. I		Preston	Index, 10/3/1903	age 61
Wright	L. B.	Illinois, 61st Infantry	Co. A	private	Preston	Index, 10/25/1888	age 63, 8/14/1904
Wyatt	Thos.	8th M.S.M. Cavalry	Co. C	private	Osceola	Index, 10/25/1888	
Young	A. J.	Illinois, 44th Infantry	Co. I	lieut.	Preston	Index, 10/25/1888	

Only Virginia and Tennessee had more skirmishes than Missouri. Under the leadership of Gen. Sterling Price and Gen. Joe Shelby.

The Mormons of Missouri, those in the Independence area had a big role for the union in the civil war which spilled over into other counties.. Hardest hit was rural areas. Their group in Hickory County was completely wiped out.

The war caused a lot of ill felling in Hickory County. Several people had moved here with their slaves. Preston community was the hardest hit. Most of these people loaded up everything including their slaves and headed back to where they had moved from. Most of them went to Arkansas because they were welcome there. This left Preston a ghost community. There were a few skirmishes in Hickory, but none major. The raiders was what did most of the damage. The soldiers only took what they needed but the guerrillas took everything and also killed. The damage by the soldiers was on their way to and from Warsaw and Springfield. The Amish community was wiped out mostly by the guerrillas and murder. In 1865 a unit got into a fight in the northeast part of the county. One soldier killed, three wounded. At Gum Springs, three confederate soldiers were killed when they stopped for some water.

The residents of Hickory County were extremely divided. It was not a matter of slaves but of states rights, It was neighbors afraid to let anyone know how they felt, even families were split over the issue. The county had a lot of unexplained killings and looting in the county. The east side of the county was the hardest hit. By the end of the war, very few homes were left. Blackened chimneys dotted the landscape, burn both sides of the lotters.

General Price's army marched through the county in 1861, the last of October. The main division cam along the old state road, western part of the county. Another division on the eastern part of the county. They met up at Yoast station south of Elkton, thirty thousand strong. It took two days for them all to pass by. Andrey J. Tillery, just past seventeen, met them at Warsaw to be their guide to Bolivar. Hickory County was in the middle of a lot of bloodshed. Although no large skirmishes in the county, it was outright killings of residents to the slaughter of prisoners by both sides. Anybody left slept with their clothes on or slept in the brush. Every night and day someone was left as a look out so the rest could be warned.

Most were poor immigrant farmers just trying to exist. Beginning to conquer their way to a more comfortable way of life. To have it all wiped out in four harsh years. But it was said of the Ozark people when the war was over and those that did live through this hell, they came home and treated each other as brothers and neighbors. Not very many that fought for the south came home as they fell in battle. In the early 1800's, a large family settled close to black oak as they called it. Their name was Mabery's from Tennessee. Things went well till the civil war broke out. John Mabery at once organized a home guard unite to fight for the south. With drilling they marched off to Springfield. When Missouri stayed in the union, Captain Mabery, came home and in very poor health, telling his four sons the fight for the north. He died a short time later. When the sons came home after the war, they found their vast holding were gone mostly because of the looters and a large amount of land had been sold for taxes. But they had an ace in the hold...the land patents. The widow of John Mabcry had kept them in her under garments. The next several years was spent in court trying to get their land back.

Somewhere between six and seven hundred Hickory County residence fought in the war. Very few that fought for the south came home. The county has more union enlistees than the south. There were a lot of strong talk by a lot of men, but they refused to put their foot where their mouth was. Most of those that had slaves in the county, sided with the north. There were some who enlisted for the south came home and reenlisted for the north. General Shelby made a Hickory County man his brigade quartermaster, John Miller. Several residents of the east side either joined the south or moved back to Tennessee or Arkansas. The best count that could be made about thirty men were killed mostly by looters in the county. The farmer was looted by both sides, mostly thought by the guerillas when the war was over they had no way to produce food in a large way. The 38,000 that came through the county was the only organized army unit to come through. In 1864 between 300 and 500 hundred guerillas was camped north of Wheatland. Prairie. They crossed the river at the ford a few miles below Hermitage. Another group went through six months later. With a few skimmers killing one man north of Preston and having some of their own wounded. This group cleaned out everything the first group had missed. A name we have found they killed north of Quincy was Albert Crouch in 1862 and James Durnell.

Chapter 7

COLORFUL MEN

THE COLORFUL MEN I HAD THE HONOR OF KNOWING IN MY LIFE TIME, THEY KEPT US LAUGHING AND VERY MUCH ENTERTAINED. I WILL USE THEIR NAMES BECAUSE THEY HAVE ALL PASSED AWAY AND WE NEED TO REMEMBER HOW THEY MADE US LAUGH WHEN WE DIDN'T FEEL LIKE IT.

These are the ones I knew in my time of life. Each one had a different way, but when they were around, they kept the crowds attention. These wonderful part of our folklore have passed on but the tales they left will remain for years. To all who knew them, their life was enriched. This is just a few of the stories and pranks. Now you be the judge. They help us to forget the hard times if but for a short while.

This is about five men that you couldn't help but like. They could tell WHOPPERS and usually did. Herb Potteroff lived southwest of Hermitage. Herb only had one arm but could swing an ax with anybody. He rolled his own smoke with one hand and no matter what tale you told, he could tell on bigger. When asked one time about the sign painted on his truck, how did he come up with a name like. Herb replied as well when I bought that one hundred acre I've found out it was nothing but a headache. Instead of aspirin. So I call it ass-born acres.

MONK EDGE WAS A TRADER. Monk was known my more people than even our Governor and when he laughed there was never a doubt who it was. Monk would say or do about anything for a good laugh. One year at a large local cattle sale, there was a newly married couple there. When the crowd got quiet, Monk at the top of his voice asked her if she was pregnant yet. Then after a short pause he said, "but I'll be she been exposed."

SHORT STATEN lived west of Pittsburg and owned the plumbing shop in Hermitage. He told one day driving the wagon and team to Pittsburg, a sudden rainstorm came up. He had a double barrel shotgun sitting up right by the side of him. Filled one barrel and the other one didn't have a drop in it. Those horses were so smart they would walk to the wagon tongue get on their side for you to hitch them up.

NYCUS FLOYD, there will never be another even close to Nycus. In things he done or stories he told. He never told a story except of himself. Nycus was a nephew of PRETTY BOY FLOYD and every year with the law leaving the area they would have a two-day family reunion and was never any trouble in Hickory County. Nycus was married to a very special lady by the name of Mable. Nobody could understand how she put up with him. Nycus was a trader mainly dogs. His old truck had stock racks with woven wire over the top and around. In the 1960's there was a national wolf hunting rendezvous in the flint hills of Kansas. Perry Reno was going with Nycus. They didn't leave Wheatland till late afternoon. Perry kept saying there won't be anywhere to pitch our tent. All Nycus would say it will be in the middle of the camp. When they topped the hill, about ten o'clock that night, camp fires covering several acres. Perry, see I told you. Nycus never said a word. Drove around and through those camp fires blowing his horn a couple of times till they got right in the middle. Sure enough was a stake, tent and bond fire marked Nycus. Perry said within one half hour several hundred men were sitting around camp fires to hear Nycus tell stories. One year coming back from a dog auction in Joplin, Nycus had to stop for gas when he went to pay for it he didn't have enough cash. He asked if he could write a check. The owner asked for his name. Nycus said FLOYD, the owner go very nervous and said I knew you was pretty boy. The gas is free, just get on down the road and I won't tell anybody you were here. He love to coon hunt. One night the dogs treed in a very large red oak, shining the light he could see two eyes. After a half box of shells, he climbed up the tree. The reason he kept missing when he got to the top, there were two one eyed coons sitting there together. Mable came home one night from work with dogs all over her. When she got out of the car, in the house "NYCUS, them dogs have to go and I don't mean next month." He loaded up about seventy-five or eighty and took off for the dog sale in Joplin. That night when Mable got home there were dogs everywhere. In response to her word of disapproval, he quietly said you didn't say not to buy any. One winter day in a café in Wheatland, loaded with coffee drinkers and two state patrolmen, the men were complaining about the snow was so deep couldn't get around. When Nycus said well it don't bother me, that old truck will go anywhere. Now Nycus, you know that old truck can't get along like a four wheel drive. Nycus came back. I'll bet ten dollars I can cross that ditch in front of the café." Which had every bit of three or more feet of snow in it. The last was seen of Nycus that day driving down 54 highway after he had crossed the ditch. Nycus had a coon dog buyer. The fellow wanted to see the dog hunt before he bought him. Nycus said now he won't tree anything but a coon. Wasn't long till the track bawl sounded went out of hearing then after here the bawl was getting faster and closer. In just a few minutes, here came a deer with the dog right behind him. Nycus said man, now there is a good dog. Getting the deer out of area where you can coon hunt. Another time he took a fellow to show off a dog. When they got to the tree where the dog was treed. No coon Nycus said well he has done it again. He beat the coon to the tree.

STANLEY PAYNE...the last of the colorful men to leave us. Stanley and Elaine farmed for many years. Sometime in the 1960's, they bought a building in Hermitage and turned it into a nice clean pool hall and café. Even the ministers were seen in there. Now Stanley was a prankster not a storyteller. Nobody ever knew what he would do next. One year while raking hay for the Chaney boys while they baled and hauled in any time he could get close enough to them to mess up the bailing or loading. He tried this one to many times all four of them got him down on the ground, took off his overalls, dumped a gun full of grease in his straddle, then put his overalls back on. The boys said you could hear him laugh two miles away while this was going on. One afternoon when Stanley lived south of Hermitage, as a neighbor was walking by the house, he heard someone hollering for help at the top of his voice. He ran to the house, yanked open the door, rushed right into the back where the bathroom was. There was Stanley holding out a towel while laughing real hard saying would you mid to dry my back. The first time I knew Stanley and Elaine was in the very early 1950's. We would get him to cut our silage each year for us. After the field was opened up, you drove along side. This kept the cutter going where it didn't stop. There was nothing be liked better than to catch you not paying close attention and blowing the cut corn on top of your head. This would always be erupted with a long hard laugh. One year a neighbor had a hundred head of steers get in our cornfield. We thought we had gotten them all out. When cutting silage, he ran the tractor right into on that had ate too much corn and died. That big calf was swelled tight ready to burst. When Stanley ran the tractor into him, he exploded. The stench was terrible. The smell stayed on that tractor till the next year. One year when he was cutting silage for us, when we came in for dinner, the ladies had the table set. When we all got washed up and came in for dinner, Stanley slipped a rubber worm in one of the tea glasses. George Riley happens to sit there. When he had drunk about half of the glass, he saw the worm. Bill Dickerson saw the worm and then everybody else. Bill trying to see in the bottom of his glass, poured the tea on the table. Stanley could take it no longer...the laughter was so hard it's a wonder we got any work done. Mother popped Stanley with the towel and said I ought to ring your neck. This brought about another round of laughter. One late afternoon, Stanley asked two little neighbor girls if they would like an ice cream cone. He came out of the house carrying two large cones. As the girls were eating them, one stopped and started turning her ice cream around. The other girl saw the fly in her sisters cone. She took her finger and began to dig in the ice cream. Stanley could keep quite no longer. He had put a rubber fly in the one. These girls thought he was a very good neighbor. Stanley had parked Elaine's car south of the café, they owned. Acting as if he was trying to get something out of the car. When two ladies came by and asked him if he was having trouble, Stanley reply was "I dropped Elaine's billfold down between the seats and now it's under the seat and I can't reach it. One of the ladies said "I'll see if I can get it for you. When she ran her arm under the seat, a scream that came forth could be heard in Wheatland. Out she pulled a black snake that Stanley had put under the seat. One year at deer season there was a group of men from the area that always went to Taney County and camped for a week. One year when the deer was not moving about, as the men came into camp that night, there were also other camps in with the one from the Hermitage area. The talk was real lively about that green horn trying to call the deer in by the same method you would call cows to the barn. Stanley joined right in the fun making of the green-horn. The Hermitage group knew it was Stanley. It is my belief Stanley went mainly for the fun. At the camp Stanley picked up an egg and proceeded to suck the egg. This grossed out some of the men and then there were some who claimed they could suck more eggs than Stanley. After Stanley consumed two dozen the others gave it up. Things like this went on all the time when Stanley was around. Then there is the story of Stanley getting a ticket in Polk County for too many fish. Stanley goes before the judge to plead his own case. His hat was what was left of a straw hat, his shirt was clean but held together with safety pins and baler twine, his overalls were clean but with baler string holding them up. What was left of them, covered most everything up. Now the most important thing was his so called shoes. Where the soles were supposed to be, was a burlap sack tied around the top of the shoe, the shoe laces, you guessed it, baler twine. All of this to hold them together. Stanley was very clean as he told the judge just getting food to feed his large family. He was clean shaven, very polite to the judge. Besides his clothes he was very presentable to the judge. The judge asked him how he pleaded, his remark was "yes judge. I had on to many fish but my family was hungry. All the meat I can get just to keep the kids from going hungry." The judge after several minutes asked Stanley to come closer to the bench. He asked Stanley if his family had enough to eat and also pay bills. Stanley response was, we get by and we don't take no handouts. The conversation between them and the judge was very timid and low. Then the judge offered Stanley some financial help which Stanley very sternly refused by saying, I take care of my family. Most of the time we keep our bellies full. We don't take charity. They could take care of themselves. The judges response was, young man, I wish we had more like you. Elaine and Stanley would give you the shirt of their back. O yeah, the judge dismissed the case.

CHEROKEE JOE...so named because his mother was a Cherokee Indian. His dad was a German. They were married in Oklahoma. Settled down on a farm. After a few years she passed away and Joe and his dad move to Pittsburg. His dad went to work for the doctor as a horse trainer. Horse racing was very big in the area. The doctor was a horse breeder and loved racing. Now Joe's father, Johannes, taught Joe everything he knew about horses. The doctor built a track on the edge of Pittsburg. Joe stayed with his father and the doctor till Johannes passed away. Joe then took over the job of training the horses. His knowledge of handling a horse spread for miles and miles around. Joe went to the horse barn one morning, there was a new colt bay with four white legs. At once Joe fell in love with tat colt, working with him all the time. After Joe took over the stable, the doctors horses were the winner or very close. Now I'm getting ahead of myself. Back in the early 1900's, horse racing was the top if not the only sport there was to enjoy. The race track at Hermitage was one to the top race tracks anywhere. Marvin Holt and his wife came to Hermitage before it was Hermitage. Their homestead was on the east side of highway 254 on south cemetery road, then to the river on east and south side. A committee was assigned to find a place for a race track, but Marvin wouldn't sell. That was just pasture land and they could use it, but whatever was built there, when they left, it belonged to him. They agreed. A first class track also the Hickory County Fair plus a rodeo was held there for many years. Marvin's house set where the Christian church parsonage now sits. The barn was about where the church is. The race track north end, was Cemetery road, west side was about one hundred feet east of his house and the barn then turning east at the edge of the tree line, then turning back south about where the row of houses are. Then on each side was built large bleachers. Of which Marvin would receive a small part of gate receipts. The race was a sell out with several people standing at every race. Now let's get back to the story...Cherokee Joe name the colt Cherokee Boy with Silver Heals. This happen while the civil war was winding down. The doctor was busy treating soldiers of both sides so everything was left up to Cherokee Joe. Disobeying the doctor's orders but slept in the loft of the barn. One night he was woken by a lot of noise. Three men were trying to steal the colt. Joe leapt out of the loft with his knife, cut the halter on the colt, knocked the man off of the horse, as he took off through the pasture. While struggling with the man, he was shot. The thieves left empty handed. In a few minutes, the family came out of the house, took Joe inside and kept him there till he was healed. They found the horse the next morning grazing in the cemetery. Little by little Cherokee Boy developed to be a very fast horse, winning every race he was entered in. they took him to the state fair in Sedalia on year and he won going away. It wasn't long till Joe's health began to fail. People of that time swore he could talk to the animals. When he started getting poorly, a meadowlark would go with him. If he went into a building, that bird would set on top of the building till Joe came out. Then fly down to his shoulder. When Joe would sit down, that bird would get as close on his shoulder as he could, put his head under his wing and go to sleep. AS time went on, Joe kept getting weaker. One day he asked one of the doctors boys if they would tell the doctor eh would like to see him. When the doctor to out to Joe's little room, the doctor said they chatted for a while then Joe reached into a drawer and pulled out a gold watch that the doctors brother had stolen years ago. Joe's remark, I pulled this off the man that tried to steal Cherokee Boy the night I got shot. I didn't want you to know it was your brother so before anyone came out of the house, I hid it in the barn. A few days later, Cherokee Joe passed away and it was told that the Meadowlark sat for several days on the tombstone.

HICKORY COUNTY: Hickory County Fairgrounds, preparing for the horse races in 1912. The fairgrounds were southwest of the Hermitage School. Picture submitted by Elsie Pitts Richards.

There was a family that was one of the most wealthiest in the county. Their name was Liggett. They built a large two story home north edge of Wheatland and a few hundred east. Mr. Liggett was also much in the politics of the county. He was an officer for the north in the civil war. He acquired large land holdings in the county. In 1864, a large ban of Guerillas came through just north of the house. A group of men under Lieutenant Paxton, engaged them in a short battle no one on either side was killed. The band moved on to a camp southeast of Preston. In about this same time. A farmer was killed while his family watched from the house. After a few minutes, one dismounted closed his eyes, laid his arms in a cross in his chest telling that they had killed the wrong person.

Just a tale about Pomme de Terre river and a road. Let's start at Black Oak and go to Hermitage long before 1850. Now it was easier to go to Urbana or Buffalo, but Hermitage was the county seat, so for any county business, you had to go to Hermitage. Not the first five and ½ miles were just fine till you came to the bluff overlooking the town and large valley below. Here you had two choices; go down this very narrow bluff, which on the north side was a very deep canyon or you could turn south cross Crane Creek, drive a mile plus west, cross at Ford and come into Hermitage from the west. If you chose to go down the narrow road on the bluff, then turn south along the river till you come to the bridge. Then after crossing the bridge, you would come on what is now the north side of the school, then on west through the few stores along the river bluff till you come to a road now marked as Indian Lane, south to edge of bluff, turn west for about two miles to what is now road 190. This will take you past the old Pleasant Hill school, bringing you out at south edge of Lucas Speedway. Now turn south till you come to intersection 254 and 83. Now turn west after a ways you will cross little Weaubleau and a few miles farther you will cross big Weaubleau. Then a little ways out of town, you will take a road south that will bring you out on the northwest side of Humansville. Now wasn't that simple to get there? One way was a long day trip. Nobody in their right minds would try to make this with being well armed, water and food. This was the way things were back in the day. Let's get back to the river…she can be a lazy stream or hell's nightmare. In 1872, the river took out a new bridge that had just been completed. In another year without much rain, local, it claimed the lives of a group of teenagers from the Galmey church. In 1951, we were down town when told the river was rising. It was coming up at a steady walk. We had a lot of shocked grain in the field. We would load as fast as we could, drive to where it hadn't got before and push the load off. Go back to get another load; we did this till the water go over the field. We felt good we saved over half our crop. Old man river wouldn't be cheated. It even got those bundles. So we spent several weeks digging the bundles of grain out of the drifts along with the copperheads.

One year when Truman Lake was backed up over some farm ground for a length of time, as soon as it went down we started plowing the first round. There were a lot of trash piled up on the back of the plow. When we went to remove that trash, it was wiggling. There were more snakes than you had ever seen in one place. I lost all my help. We did not get off the tractor to the ground. We drove up close to the road and got off on to the truck. I couldn't guess how many copperheads we killed.

Chapter 8

RAMBLING MIND... PUSHING A PEN

WHY!! I'm asked, what do you hope to gain by taking the time to do this. The answer to why is as I began to do some research into stories and happenings in the county, there was no stopping place. I could find bits and pieces here and there. I remember as a young lad, some of the wild tales I heard older men talk about and just what I thought they were. Just mighty tall yarns, but when I dug into history, most of them are recorded as true. Some of those tales cannot be put on paper, because too gross. I was lucky enough to live in a time when old men sat and whittled and spit and talked. A time when they were told stories by their peers. Not wrote down but repeated by each generation. A time when this area was first settled. The good and bad times. If not recorded somewhere, will be lost forever. Several of the stories may be listed somewhere else, but to repeat them is not the end of the world. ALL HAVE come from my involvement with my kin folk or at the whittlers bench. One person would start a tale and another would join right in to give more details somewhere in this two hundred year old history. Much of it has been lost. Yes, some of those tales were hard to swallow but these story tellers would swear by them. A tale about a hoop snake. They would roll into a circle and with a sharp hard tail, drive that into their prey to paralyze it. Then there is the joint snake. I would come apart in joints. One year while digging post holes in a swamp area, we hit a snake with brown with white markings and you could pull it apart just like a snap connection. So I know that story is true. I had always thought they were just pulling my leg. Several species of fish and animals have disappeared over the years. The would tell stories of large herds of deer, elk, bison, with also an abundance of black bears, mountain lions, timber wolfs, turkey, quail, prairie chickens, catfish so big one man couldn't handle it, honey bees so thick there was wax used for wagon axel grease. Hickory County was in with several other counties that offered a bounty of two dollars for mountain lions and fifty cents for wild cats. Huge trees so big that by the time saw mills came into the county, walnut was used for siding or piled into piles to burn so a field could be farmed. The county was very well stocked with wild and tame animals till the civil war broke out. The soldiers took from the farmers what they needed, but the guerrillas looted and killed at random. After the war was over, several years the cities were in the roaring twenties. The rural communities were begging to get back to having things a little better. With prohibition, the rule of the land still was as some would claim the backbone of the recovery, moonshine making and running was an everyday business of the county. When wall street fell, it was hardly noticed for a while. Then along came the dust bowl. Now the rural community was in trouble. You would hear of horror stories about the people in the southwest going to the barn and getting lost and dying, just a few feet from the barn or house, because they couldn't see on foot in front of them. They would tell for the dirt being so thick in the house it would even fill the sugar and salt bowls. Even if they were wrapped in cloth. The dirt was so moved about even fences were coved up till you couldn't find the fence. The exodus to California, left the bread basket with very few farmers left in the Midwest.

Yes the old men told some whoppers maybe not all true, but we listened for every word. As young lads you believed everything. Well at least you wanted to believe and dream of all that was told. With wood shaving and tobacco juice mix together, mothers now days would go in hysterical to think of her baby sitting in that mess and hearing those awful tales. In the age of time

I'm writing this in 2014, we have lost the world of just sitting and listening or visiting. We no longer have time for stuff like that. Now we must keep up with the JONES', whoever they are. If you think I'm wrong, let someone get a new truck or tractor. Not long till more are in the neighborhood. The lake (Pomme de Terre) has brought in a lot of new people. There was a time when you knew everyone in the county and several around, but we are all dying off and new people moving in. The traffic has got so back, you may need to wait tem minutes to get on the highway. And it is a regular site to see five or six cares in a mile. I'm on the opinion, when you can see your neighbors chimney smoke, the neighbors are close. When my wife and I bought this place, we didn't have a neighbor within two miles. And that was our son and daughter-in-law. Now we have sole some off to our grandkids and that is too close. Even if it is a fourth mile away. In the dying age, as I like to refer to this time, our young people are losing the work ethic and the self-respect and the love of our savior. The question? Who's fault is it? In my opinion, it is on the parents shoulders. Very few parents us the scripture. I Proverbs where it says, "spare the rod and spoil the child. Or even teach ourselves, let along the children the BIBLE and it's wisdom.

The towns are in a lackluster stage of growth, the big boom the county that several of the residents expected with the building of the dam. Yes there has been a moderate growth mostly with retired people who just want to take it easy and enjoy life. Some of these are hard to get acquainted with as not in the socializing mood. Very few that I have got to know are not cranky, hard to get along with. Some even have a what can I do to make some life better for someone. Our county could be described as a bedroom county. Very few jobs in the county and most all farms have had to enlarge to stay in operation. So a lot fewer residents in the rural part of county.

As we come to the end as Paul Harvey would say on his radio broadcast, NOW FOR THE REST OF THE STORY. The opry house in Pittsburg held a large attraction for some years. Bill Ring was the Emcee on several occasions, along with Slim Wilson, Junior Hayworth, Aunt Marther, the Carter family, which included June who later married Johnny Cash. These also appeared with Red Foley on the Ozark Jubilee.

We spoke earlier of the large mining around Pittsburg, as well as the rest of the county. The mineral didn't play out. There was a lot of lead, zinc and barite left. It just cost too much to get it to a smelter. The railroad hadn't made it to the county yet and the ore had to be transported by wagon to get the ore where it could be shipped to a smelter. Old timers claim there is lots of ore in them there hills. On my farm there is a shaft about thirty feet deep that barite was hauled up from.

WHEATLAND TORNADO, FRIDAY, MAY 25, 1917

A DIFFERENT VERSION THAT WAS RECORDED OF THE TORNADO NORTH OF WHEATLAND.

It was 8:45 in the afternoon in the northwest corner of Wheatland, when a very calm day turned violent. The path of a terrible storm went in a northeast direction. The tract was about a hundred yards wide, laying everything flat on the ground, no matter the size. A lot of large trees tore out by the roots. No one could believe what they saw, splinters and straw driven into posts of trees as if you bored a hole and placed them in as if you then filled the hole back up so you couldn't tell. Clouds began to build and turn color about 4:00 and back in the southwest the clouds were as black as black could get. The people told later you could hear a rumbling in the southwest as it moved closer. The closer it got, the louder it sounded. The clouds very ugly, but a beautiful fireworks in the sky, the lightening was putting on. With much fear, the people wondered what was going to happen. They had never seen anything like this before. This kind of weather was new to them. As it got closer, the noise got much louder, the sky turned a greenish color. I'm sure some of them thought the end of the world had come. At first just the roofs were taken off northwest of town, as it moved farther northeast. The next morning, only splinters could be seen where once nice buildings had stood. The floor was left undamaged, but with terrible damage how could this be. A shoe in a tree. Mrs. Bandel was found sitting on a feather bed way out in the timer. Mr. Bandel a very large man, three hundred pounds or more, was found in a branch across the road laying down. He passed away the news June, 1918. Lamon, the Bandels son, was blown across the road. He didn't know anything had happen till the hard rain was hitting him in the face, waking him up. Leonard Bandel lived about a half mile north from his parents. He was building a two story house. The storm picked it up and carried some distance away and laid it on its side. The next year, Leonards wife and two small children past away. What chickens were left, had no fathers on them. After the storm Leonard with his family, including a two month old baby, started for his parents place. It rained so hard, they thought they were going to drown. Several people said they had never seen it rain so hard. The Sr. Bandels also lost a daughter the next year. She had a nice dresser set that could not be found. The next year it was found along with several pictures of the Bandels and some papers in the woods, next to summer cemetery. Next farm was Harry Bennett's, two miles south. Just one mile south of what is now Y Highway. The house and smoke house was left intact. The barn just east of the house was carried a forth mile and scattered over a field. The house was moved eight feet off of foundation, breaking out all windows. Every tree in the orchard was pulled out by the roots. An apple tree close to the house, was blown into the kitchen window. The storm lifted the cook stove and table up and placed the tree underneath. In the living room, a lighted lamp fell on the floor, but somehow put out the light and didn't break the lamp. Seth Bennett, a nephew, was in bed upstairs and slept through it all. He was woken by an excited aunt. They had to crawl out through the window, not a door could open. Cleo laid a three month old baby in the tree branch while she crawled out. The rain was so hard the water was ankle deep in the yard. Not a shingle left on the house. Everything in the house, dishes on the floor. The day before Cleo had baked bread and put the loaves in large glass bowls set on the table. She had also strained two crocks of milk. Those loaves were found the next day in the milk and swelled so large they couldn't pull them out of the bowls. The children had a pet pig in a box in the house. When they found the pig, it was still in the box not hurt. A mare and colt was in the barn lot, could not be found anywhere, till a neighbor came from two miles away leading them home. Cleo and 156 hens. They picked up 146 dead ones. The storm continued its path, but with less damage. Tore complete roofs off buildings and in one house, drove a sliver of wood just over the top of a baby bed. A tornado hit Cross Timbers May 1, 1948. A lot of damage was done and destroyed twenty-five barns and sever small buildings in the countryside.

Chapter 9

CRIME AND KILLINGS

The first legal hanging in Hickory County, was a guilty verdict by a jury for murder, was in 1845. In 1900, a fellow by the name of Poor Killed John Adams, four and one half miles south of Elkton, with an ax then threw his body into a hole of water. Then a few days later came back, got his body and put it in the back of his wagon. He drove around with the body in the wagon bed. It began to attract flies and gave off an odor. He was arrested at Warsaw after bones were found in a brush pile. John Adams' body is buried in Hermitage Cemetery. The date on the stone reads "John Adams, November 2, 1900–June 21, 1901. Poor again was arrested near Fairfield where he and his wife were camping. There was still blood on the wagon bed floor. He was tried by the court in Humansville and given a sixty year sentence. For some reason, he was released in 10 years. A lynch mob formed to hang him but his father convinced them to let the law handle the problem. Several years later he applied for a pension then when the case was brought before the court, again he claimed it was self-defense.

Bill Brown killed his brother Tom in 1897, while they were picking corn. The team took the body to the house with Tom's body in the wagon. Bill was given life sentence in 1948. He died in the state pen.

Gluson Bybee was killed at Cross Timbers in 1934, by George Ussery. He was sent to the pen for a few years.

A freak accident in 1917, when a two year old boy was riding in the spring seat of the wagon while his parents picked corn. They looked up and he was laying down in the seat, thinking they had fallen asleep. They kept on picking till they got a wagon load. When they climbed into the wagon, they couldn't wake him up. Then they got frantic. Now this was about noon, thinking they had hit him in the heat with an ear of corn. They got him to the doctor as quick as possible. After the doctor examined him, he told the parents he had been hot in the head. Somehow sometime that morning a stray bullet had hit him. His name was T.J. Canthon.

In 1942, Merle Clark, about fourteen years, was taking a shotgun out of a car barrel first. The gun went off blowing a hole in his stomach. He was the son of Wesley and Marie Clark of Hermitage.

George Dixon was killed in 1847 by John Shanson, two and one half miles north of Wheatland. He escaped, went to California, stayed there for twenty years, came back to Wheatland and was never arrested. No one left living to testify against him.

Bill Dollarhide was shot by Ray Moore in Hermitage, on the square. No charges filed.

A prank that turned deadly. In a model T, going down Brass Hill west of Hermitage, Billie Donovan was complaining about the driving. The driver took the steering wheel off of the steering post and said well let's see you do any better. He died on the way to the doctor's office. He was 16 years old.

Elloworth Fields shot George Homer in a dispute over wages owed to him. He got ninety days in the county jail.

Jim Gardner was shot and killed by a law officer three miles east of Elkton, for robbing a bank in 1917.

Frank Huffman the outlaw, was killed by John Pitts, about one mile south of Cross Timbers, in 1894. Robbing for several years, the law had been trying to capture him. He had a nice reward on his head. Huffman was shot for the reward by one of his own men. They were going to rob a store that night. Pitts collected the reward and moved to Oklahoma where he was killed later.

Bill McCarlin was sheriff in 1899. He went to arrest Westester Relford. He shot at the sheriff, the bullet missed and went through the horse neck. The horse lived. Relford went to the pen for twenty years.

Sameal Naffyinger was killed northwest of Wheatland in 1875. There had been hard feelings between him and Dick Rogers for several years.

Orval Paxton was killed north of Wheatland in the house, where the Amish saw mill is now. He was shot through the window. A few minutes after he put his two little nieces down off his lap. It was always believed his father-in-law done the shooting, but could never prove it. This was done in 1922.

John Carsoll was killed at the courthouse door in 1860 by sheriff Pitts.

Guy Ponell was killed one and one half miles east of Wheatland on the old road that takes off 54 at the highway barn. He was killed by Frank Crutainyer.

P.O. Proper's bones were found two and one miles northwest of Flemington in 1956, in Bill George's pasture. He had disappeared four months earlier. It was believed he shot himself, but no one knew for sure. A gun was found several yards from the body.

Ira Quigy was killed at Wheatland in 1892, by Sigel Paxton. He was put under bond, then was caught in the warehouse owned by John Imus. He was shot in a shoot-out by law officers.

Jack Sally was killed at Cross Timbers in 1901, by Tom Heath. They had a grudge for three or four years. Mr. Heath had lost his mind. He died in the asylum.

Stiltz Lyman killed Tom Moore at Quincy 1898. He was sent to the penitentiary for five years.

Bill Wilson was killed at Quincy in 1874. Stiltz Lyman was tried for his murder, but the law couldn't prove it.

Olie Cooper was shot two times from behind, killing him instantly, February 18, 1984. The killer was waiting in ambush for him. Earl Romesburg was later arrested. They had a long standing feud. He was tried and convicted. He served life in the pen.

Brad Barber was killed by Bob Fletcher in 1847, over a poker game on the north edge of the square in Wheatland.

Billy Bigler was killed at Elkton in 1878, by constable Lige White, while trying to arrest him.

Henry Clark was killed or if he killed himself in 1930, near Dooly Bend. He was in jail and just walked away. He went to his home. It was never known whether the officers killed him or he killed himself.

Vernon Halbert shot Hase Litttral, three and one half miles west of Pittsburg. It didn't kill him, but it was a year before he could be up and around.

George Hickman shot at Tom Williams at Cross Timbers. Didn't hit Tom, but the bullet struck Don Miller's wife, in 1924. She recovered.

Eva Hicks was found choked to death near Pleasant Ridge Church. Her father was brought back from Colorado for the crime. He was charged, but no convicted. Another sister to Eva, turned him in because she thought she could get his money.

Homer Johnson was found dead with the back of his head caved in, southwest of Pittsburg in 1916. Never knew who killed. It was always believed to be his older brother.

Bill Jorden cut Jim Blackwell with a knife near the well on the square in Hermitage in 1903. Jim Blackwell recovered.

Charlie Mann was killed in 1906, by Zeke Cox. Mr. Mann had set up all night with his sick wife. He had gone to the doctors house to get some medicine for her. He had to wait for the doctor to get home. He was so sleepy, he laid down under a tree to wait. The constable and Mr. Cox went for him. When he was awaken, he scared Cox so bad, Cox hit him with a baseball bat.

Tom Mashburn was killed at Elkton in 1891, by Billie Beck. Mashburn, a young lad had been bullying Beck for some time. This time in church he began to tease and bully him again, so Beck pulled out a pistol and shot him.

Nathan Pippens lived southeast of Preston. Tom Morgan's father was at a dance at the Pippen's farm. Trouble arose on the outside of the house. One man was shot. He slipped upstairs without being detected. The blood dripped through the upstairs floor to the dance floor. He had laid there and bled to death. No name is recorded who he was. This happened during the civil war.

Ben Ollinger was killed by Sherm McCracken or his wife, in about 1891, south of Dooly Bend, four and one half miles. They had trouble over digging a well. McCracken didn't want to pay him for helping him to dig the well.

Siglo Paxton was shot in 1893. Him and John Carter were fishing ten miles north of Wheatland, in Round Bottom (in Breshears valley). John Carter jumped out of the boat into the river. Siglo was shot three times. Nobody ever knew who it was that shot Mr. Paxton and hill him. Mr. Carter was scared to death, but not hurt.

Tim Wright's father Oscar Wright, shot Henry Knoll three miles east of Cross Timbers. He was shot three times. Wright hit one of the barrels of Knoll's shot guns, cutting it off eight inches in front of the hammer, bent the rod between barrels. One shot entered his right shoulder of Knoll's He shot another time in the back of the shoulder. When they dug the bullets out, they went in three inches. Mr. Knoll claimed he never could figure out why Mr. Wright was mad.

Clyde Bain was accidentally killed in Kansas City, when the police mistook him for a fugitive. He grew up in Hickory county in the 1940's.

Will Buckner, 1894, either hung himself or was strung up by a bunch of men from Bolivar.

Jake Stokes and Ed Brown were fighting over a girl, Sarah Creasy at Union School, west of Elkton, in the 1980's. She ran between them. Ed Brown cut her in the face, though one eye and through her mouth.

Graft Robinson killed Dr. Dickey, 3 miles west of Pittsburg, by hitting him on the head with a rock.

Bob Hito was killed by person's unknown at Quincy sometime before 1900.

Sig Reser and Amos Lindsey, were brother-in-laws, fighting. Lindsey cut Reser across the abdomen. He walked about a quarter of a mile holding his guts in Dr. Stewart cleaned the grime off, sewed him up and he lived for several years in the 1890's.

Liva Rule left Elkton about 1894 and went to Oklahoma, got in a fight, throat was cut from ear to ear and died.

Olay Mashburn found a man floating in a treetop on Ida Adae's farm at Pomme de Terre river. Nobody could identify the body, so he was buried in a hole of water, which was about 35 feet deep. This happened in the 1890's. At this time of period, it was legal. This is now just below where the Pomme de Terre Dam is.

Gip Huffman killed a man by the name of Feltenbarger. He went to the pen and died there in the 1980's.

Carrol Pitts was killed by a posse at the courthouse door for horse stealing.

For some time there had been bad blood between Thomas Allen (marshal) and the Clayton boys. Charlie Clayton standing in front of the drug store in Wheatland, when Mr. Allen walked by. Charlie asked the marshal if he wanted to arrest him. The marshal, replied, "yes, if you don't be quiet." Clayton turned around into the store yelling and waving his stick. The marshal followed him into the store, pulled out his revolver and ad he fired the first shot, Clayton took his stick, knocked the gun up. As the marshal fell backwards, he fired twice more, both hitting their mark. Clayton still following, turned into the butcher shop, where he fell and died. When Will and Ed learned Clayton had been killed, one got a pistol and the other a shotgun, loaded with buckshot. They found him in another store. The marshal raised his pistol, but it wouldn't fire. As her ran out the back door, Will opened up on him with his pistol. Ed fired as the marshal ran across the street with both barrels. One ball hit him in the back of the head and others in the shoulder. At a hearing in the courthouse in Hermitage, all charges against both parties were dismissed.

SOCIALIST ASSESMENT

1938 the resident of the county were backward, very poorly educated, very evasive, somewhat timid and in an unexplained way, though very tough, they had to be to live in this hostile environment.

That was the way it came to me after reading Mr. West's book Plainville U.S.A., though I do not agree with his assessment. Since this is 2014, I lived those years. No we didn't have any money, we were very rich in what makes man feel like he has the bull by the tail on a downhill pull. I guess what I'm trying to say, we had time for life to enjoy our neighbors and the wonders of GOD'S CREATION. There were very few people with let's say within thirty miles, you did not know and also they were like neighbors. Now in 2014, you speak to a stranger, they look at you, what are you up to fellow. Now let us get down to what I got out of Plainville U.S.A., which is Wheatland. He uses no names that are correct, but any resident can figure it out. I would encourage you to read this book and also the one wrote fifteen years later called Plainville Revisited.

Somewhere in 1938 to 1939, a professor from MU, I think, was traveling through the Midwest looking for a town where the people were less connected to the outside world. It was his object to study these people; live with them for a while, get to know them and study their culture. It all came by accident that he chose Wheatland or maybe GOD intervened. Whatever the reason, his car broke down just outside of Wheatland. It was take to Bill at Darby's garage, to have it fixed and found out it was going to take several days. So he and his wife got a room at the hotel. Cleaning up he moseyed on down to the square where several elderly, sat chewing, whittling and talking. As soon as he walked up to them, they claimed up. He was a stranger. He might be some sort of government spy sent to see just what they were doing and maybe a revenuer. This is what he was told once he got someone's confidence. After the second day, he said to his wife "we have found what we have been looking for." When he publish the number one book, it was used for studies in all colleges across the U.S.

FOR STUDING RURAL AMERICA. Many people thought we had been portrayed wrong, but it was good to think we had made national status. But no one knew who we were. After a few days, one elderly gentleman began to open up to him. Now he knew it was the right place. After several more days spent on the square and telling he was a writer from M.U. he was a last accepted. He wrote several stories about Hickory called Woodland, Wheatland Plainville, Hermitage Discovery, Weaubleau Straton, Bolivar Liberty, Springfield Large Town, K.C. Metropolis. All families that he wrote about, kept a double record and I don't think any persons real name should be recorded here. The only family's real name to be used, because he was the first white man to cross Pomme de Terre when it was release from keeping the white man going onto Indian land. Their names were Jones. They staked off one hundred and sixty acres. The location sweet springs is Gum Springs. They were a very rough family. There was very little law at this time in history.

Chapter 10

A SOCIAL PROFESSOR VIEW

In 1938 a man and wife searching for something, but they didn't where to look found what they were looking for by accident or maybe it was divine guidance. I'm not to judge. The book he wrote name Plainville U.S.A., is about backward people, the poor, the misguided, the uneducated, the total different kind of living that there were in Woodland County (HICKORY). I disagree on a lot of the assessment he made in his book and some will argue with. But who am I to not agree with what he wrote. I'm just one of those bullheaded ridge running Ozark hillbillies. Yes, we were poor. We had just began to tame these hills and valleys. But we didn't know we were poor. Everybody was just like the next person. We had only one class of people, we thought. WE are told in the good book, love your neighbor. Well, who is your neighbor. When you go to town now, everybody is a stranger. I lived in the time he wrote about and I saw things a little different. There within twenty miles, you knew just about everyone by their first name. if hardships fell on someone, people came for miles around to do what needed to be done. It was not unusual to see ten to twenty men helping while the wives brought the food and prepared it. So what do I know? I don't have much book sense. But through these years, all I've wound up with is horse sense. Now there I go again, rambling on instead of sticking. As a song writer wrote a song a few years ago. That's my story and I'm sticking to it.

Mr. West and his wife had left their college a few days ago looking for something, but didn't know where they would find it. Even they didn't know if they would find the right one. They had been on the roads in the Midwest and thought we are no closer to what we're looking for. Their car broke down close to Wheatland. Upon getting the car to Bill Darby's garage and finding out it would take three days before it would be fixed. So they just tried to make the best of a bad situation. They went to the hotel just a stone's throw away. Mr. West got cleaned up and went down to the square where several elderly men were sitting, spitting, chewing, whittling, and telling stories. As soon as Mr. West walked up, the talking stopped. They had him figured out. "Yep, he sure enough a government man." Mr. West visited a little while, but remarking he broke down while in this area and wouldn't get fixed for a few days. The next day there they were, doing the same thing. By the stroke of luck, he gained the trust of one elderly gentleman in town. HE explained to what he was and who he was. In the next few hours, he had all the stories he could handle at one time. He went back to his room, told his wife he thought he had found what they were looking for. The next day the elderly gentleman and introduced him and what he was after. Still they didn't not fully trust him. After several weeks of spending days and nights at any function, the people began to open up to him. At first, he was not trusted when he wrote in front of them. He would need to go back to his hotel to write the information down. As time went on, the people had become more relaxed around him.

Now, he will try to set the double manuscript. He had to keep the location and names of everybody disclosed. "I will disclose the places; Woodland County (Hickory), Plainville (Wheatland), Discovery (Hermitage), Straton (Weaubleau), Liberty (Bolivar), Large Town (Springfield) Metropolis (KC).

Very few family names will I reveal. If I know except for one and the only reason I will mention them, is because they were the first white man to cross legal. They had staked out their claim the day before so make it legal, they were the first ones to cross the Pomme de Terre river. The two men went by the name of Jones. Mr. West called the name of the place Sweet Springs. The amount of land they staked out was 160 acres. This was a very rough family, broke no laws, but also without any law they had to make their own law. As a rule they were left alone and left others alone.

Plainville, how he received the people, very poor and backward. What he couldn't see was, the slow pace was what most people wanted. A few people had been to that hustle and bustle kind of life and was not ready for it yet. We liked going once every week or two just to mingle with the crowd in town, stayed all day, go to a movie show or sit and listen to the, as we called them, old men, run off on tale after tale, till your sides hurt so bad from laughing. The neighbors helping one another with whatever they needed. I've lived in the time fifteen to twenty men would gather to fetch in the crop or cut the winter wood. If a man was laid up for a spell, the woman would bring fix'ins and everybody had a good visit.

We don't do that anymore. Even our talk has changed. There are times we are losing some of our rich heritage. The first trip my wife made was to the Mayo Clinic. The nurse came in and began to tell us what to expect. As soon as she stopped talking, my wife said, "boy you people up here sure do talk funny." That nurse burst out laughing and said "no honey, it's you who talks funny." After that we were on first name basis.

The history he left us (PLAINVILLE USA) with, is a treasure very valuable to the area. Yes, it upset some people when the book came out. Recognized all over the US as a master piece, but at the same time, upsetting to our uppity-de mucky. Yes, I will agree some of it portrayed things wrong, but it's the way he saw them as from the outside. He wrote openly about the good things and also the good times. But also of the bad not only people, but things that happened. In his opinion Woodland County was a backward county was a backwood rural community of which was more prominent rural than counties with a large city. He did not see it as a closed county, but the people were poor and leading a much slower type of life. Now to me this was great for we got to experience a way of life that is gone forever. Our children and on down the line will never have that great opportunity to listen to old set of men blow while whittling. Or sit on a quiet creek bank with a cane or hickory pole. To lay back and dream of becoming a cowboy, chairman of company, we all dream of being a millionaire. Or even President. But in this hurry up and get there type of living, our children are missing out on the good time we had in our time. Woodland County was growing very little except for a very few people looking for cheap land and of course those that are up to no good. Woodland has no large cities. At the time, Mr. West wrote Pittsburg was the largest town in Woodland County, due to the rich deposit of zinc and lead. Neither did he regard the type of living the people had. It was more suited to their culture and more or less satisfied with a slower way of life. The way I understand the book, Mr. West cannot understand why the people didn't accept the new way of life that the large city people enjoy.

The express how fast time has changed residents in Hickory rural parts of the county. Electricity didn't come available till early 1950, thanks to R.E.A. Then rural life began to bloom. We also seen large improvements in the availability of products, house appliances, and machinery. Because of the veterans back in the work place the demand for everything exploded. We were at last humming. To explain how much time has changed. My grandmother came here with her family as a young girl in a covered wagon to homestead land. Then in the 1960's boarded a jet in KC airport and flew to Arizona to see her sister and also a man land on the moon. Now don't tell me we are still dumb and backward.

Chapter 11

PLAINVILLE REVISITED

Research fifteen years later by Mr. Gallaher Jr. In using the first book on Plainville, Mr. Gallaher Jr., wanted to study the change if any was in Woodland County. In his observation, quite a few changes had evolved. The people as in the first book, were suspicious of his intents. It took several weeks before he gained their trust. The living habits had changed. The Saturday day and night was not near as large at plain view. The prosperous times had afforded rural residence to go to larger towns to shop. The dress code had in a very short time went from one extreme to almost in the other way. Women were showing lots of skin, most boys were now wearing Levi's, hair trimmed, slicked down and more bold. The boys thought they had to have a car to hang in and date. The girls were trying to rid themselves of long dresses ugly socks and use a little make up.

Most families still had large gardens canned most of their food had their own milk, cow butchered their own meat. Anyone not doing these things were considered lazy. In better terms as you would hear someone say "he's not worth a grain of salt". Most of the clothes the women and girls wore were still from feed sacks as well as the guys shirts. It was totally unheard of for the man to get the feed without his wife to pick out the pattern of sack she wanted. Families still hunted and went fishing, but now for meat and relaxation. If you had a good hunting dog, you were living in high part of the hog in your neighborhood. Everybody that had a late model shotgun or dog was living right. There was a rich prestige to have an exceptional dog even an outstanding horse. Now this fellow could be even of the riff-rat and still for this one quality, was looked upon with pleasing eyes. As was recorded in the second book, if the girl or boy wasn't married by the time they were thirty years old, they were called old maids or bachelors.

There are reports that the older women would complain about the younger generation so much, the sheriff would remove the firing pin from their gun to keep them from hurting someone.

One elderly man shot the radiator of a group of boys that were pestering him. The dad wanted the gentleman arrested. The sheriff and the neighbors thought he had his rights. The boys had kept busy harassing the gentleman by making the horn stick on his pickup. Next time turning all the lights on the truck, even went as far as to turn his large stack of wood over, that was neatly stacked.

It is now noted that most large families are a thing of the past. Most couples wait a few years before starting a family. This is made possible by contraceptives. Most women now use a doctor for pre-med care. Very few midwives are used. It's noted that most babies are now bottle fed. Very few mothers breast fed because to live higher on the hog, the wife must find work off the farm.

In the first book of Plainville, it was noted that parents was the only thing needed to teach children about honesty, respect, obedience, morality, and financial ethic. These are still used by most parents, but rely more on education. Now it's college for those who can afford it. Now the cost of a public college for tuition, will run about $3,000 a semester.

In the first book you would hear a parent say when they would tell you how they would discipline their children. We would whoop the hell out of them. Now the modern parent has read Dr. Spock's book on how to raise a child. I really doubt he had any of his own. No wonder the younger are getting into more trouble and don't have the moral or work standers of their parents.

Mr. West refers to the Ballou family, who we call Breashears, as the oldest and largest in the county and was also a closed community. You was welcome, but if you were not a relative, you couldn't live there. Mr. Gallaher states the settlement was once very large by conservatives. There were at one time over five hundred in the valley. Now much of the family has disappeared. But it is still very prominent in the county. The disbursement was caused by two things, but connected to each other. A bridge was built over the Pomme de Terre river on the west side and also a better road on both sides of the river to connect Wheatland to Fairfield. This was a swinging bridge. A lot of the ancestors are still here, but no concentrated in one area and it is almost impossible to meet someone today that is not related to the Breashears tree. This is how much a large clan can have upon an area. And may I add, on hundred sixty plus years later, influence is still strong and well respected.

In 1942 there were thirty six rural county schools. In 1954, the county had consolidated in to the five large town schools.

Perhaps, the largest objection from the residents when a form of government intervention can that was called a GAME WARDEN. They were to be located in Woodland County. No one would rent his family a house. He wound up buying one in Hermitage. The landlords had been threatened by some prominent people not to rent to him and these were law bidding citizens. It took several years before he was accepted by a majority of the people. The main reason is one person put it, he would arrest his own mother. This came about when his wife one day caught a huge bass before the season opened. He made her throw it back. Her remark was and I had to marry a damn game warden. Another time the couple who they hung around with a lot, he arrested for having an illegal deer in their freezer.

The greatest event or opinion in reading PLAINVILLE REVISITED, was the conception that the social attitude had changed, now with modern technology being more readily accepted by the rural community in attitude. The hill people are not looked down on. As one gentleman put it, get on board or get THE HELL OUT OF THE WAY. They even let electricity to be put in their homes and then they had to have thinks like electric ice boxes, radios, washing machines, even a contraption to milk the cows. But worse of all, was the new light bulbs that will cause you go blind.

To survive the farms, you had to get larger or go out of farming. So the county, as all, other had to get into a bidding war to survive. Old farmers sold out to younger farmers or those who could afford the debt. The people that sold out either moved to town or to a larger city to find work. Within a very short time, there were one half of the farms left and at time went on, even less. The extension office stated that we are in our last generation of marginal farms. Even those that relied upon the timber to make a living, was giving it away, as many people now had gas to heat and cook with. Pine timber was brought in by the railroad was much easier to build with than our native lumber. As one man said I could cut enough wood to supply the whole town and still not enough to make a living.

Between the two books on PLAINVILLE USA from 1938 to 1940, for the first book and 1954 to 1955 for the second book, he writes he sees a large contrast in the way the people think and live. The first book speaks about the people in the hills (live lack animals) in my observation and in visiting the so called hill people, it was not by choice in a lot of cases. But just to accept the fact it was forced up on them. They did the best they could to survive till times got better. As one family put it we were happy and did not fret over what we couldn't help. After all, there was no work anywhere due to the depression. Now that times are good, we are doing better.

The first book spoke of dialects hard to understand. We were a land of new immigrants into one culture. Some of the people spoke very little English. By the time of the second book, our children went to school. WE had come out of the great depression. Then the second world war, everybody left from the war had a good job. As the young men returned, the economy was humming. A lot of demand for new products. New roads were to be built, house construction could not get enough carpenters. Thus being strangers in a new type of world seeing how the rest of the world lived. Then next came huge improvements in communication and transportation.

In the end of PLAINVILLE TWO, he concluded we were not much different than anyone else. Since the war had resettled, a lot of people and roads crisscross. The county with a lot of residents driving to other places. He can't decide if we had caught up with the rest of the world or has it caught up with PLAINVILLE IN WOODLAND COUNTY.

Chapter 12

STORIES THAT GO IN EVENTS THAT I MISSED

One of the most widely fun events happened when a couple got married. It was a SHIVAREE, all kinds of things happened. A few nights after they were married very late, the object was to surprise them with lots of shotgun firing. Anything to make a loud noise. And this could happen several times within a month. And they had better have lots of candy and cigars. I've seen young teenagers get so sick, they thought they were going to die from smoking a cigar at the event. What did the people do? Well I will list a few without any names. One time a town doctor was with us carrying a pair of hip rubber boots. This shivaree started earlier than usual. About the time it was going to break up, the doctor said not yet. We all got a hold of the fellow, put the boots on him, tied them tight about eight inches below his straddle, filled each leg up to the top of the boot with ice and sat there for about two hours. Took the boots off and the doctor remarked he better behave his self tonight. Salt was always sprinkled on the bed sheets. If they lived in town, they would put the new bride in a wheel barrow and the groom would push it around town with everybody making enough even the dead rose. Another time one of my classmates married a fellow ten miles from Hermitage, OUT OF CIGARS, so after midnight some time we tied him up took him to a very remote part of the county, rough holler about eight miles from where they lived. Took all his clothes off except his underware, untied him dumped him in the river and left him. No shoes, no clothes and all wet he was a very good sport. We could laugh about that for years. Remember them days? There was no such thing as cell phones.

The Pomme de Terre dam construction started in 1957 and finished in 1964. The Corps of Engineer had made a bad boo-boo. They built the dam, closed the gates and hadn't built a bridge across the Lindley arm. The lake rose to the poll stage. Nobody could get from the Pittsburg side, north. Things got a little heated. They began to let water out to lower the river as fast as possible, causing hardship on anybody downstream. For us to complain, was like talking to Mt. Rushmore. My wife was working in town. We had three small children. For her to get to work, my father would meet her on the other side of the creek. When it was back up, we would row across with three small children every morning and night the two older ones, though this was fun, this lasted for several weeks. Most of our land was under water, no field work was done till the water went down.

Round bottom waterfall is in Breshears valley, about one and one half miles south of the Mastodon dig (Boone Springs). This is a fourteen foot fall form a limestone bluff head of a large ravine.

January 1885, the sheriff went to Humansville on the twenty-third to arrest Kahoka for murder, committed twenty-two years earlier. At the printing of this article, the verdict has not yet been reached.

July 5, 1917, a buggy arrived from Humansville to pick up Dr. Allen (dentist). Soon the buggy was headed back to Humansville. Somewhere between Wheatland and Hermitage, a man blocked the road carrying two 44 revolvers. His partner slid off of his horse, collected the money and all the articles.

In 1887, Hickory County was about to get a railroad. Two surveys were laid out from Clinton to Bolivar. The western route was chosen because it cost less to build. Wheatland had a thriving business, but the cost of laying the tracts was much less to go through Weaubleau. When this was settled a boom effect hit Weaubleau. Tents were first put up till a building could be constructed. Weaubleau population exploded to well over five hundred in a very short time. February 22, 1906, the first car arrived in Wheatland. The people in the car stayed all night in the hotel. Soon large crowds gathered to look at the contraption. Finally one young man reached out to touch it. He even got enough nerve to sit on its fenders. This story was front page new in the local paper. The driver of the car was Peter Serivener.

There were several recipes for moonshine. Here is one that was printed in the local paper...Gather some hops into a ten gallon can. Also one bag of bug poison, one quart of axel grease, one bar of lye soap. Boil mixture for 38 hours and strain through a large sock. Then to each pint, add one grasshopper to give it some KICK.

In 1904, Wheatland population grew to over 500. In the early 1840's and 50's, the county was in grave financial trouble. The government was issuing paper money which the people had no faith in and for good reason. Very few businesses would honor paper money. If your paper money was from another state you were out of luck. Each state made their own money. Even some banks printed their own money. Cows sold for five dollar paper money or twenty dollars if gold or silver.

Some funny pranks??? The 1940's, old Charley Benedict had as garage on the southeast corner of the square in Hermitage. Now Charlie didn't hear so good. Tow ladies stopped for gas and asked Charlie if he had a restroom. Charlie thought they asked for a wisk broom. His reply was JIST BACK UP HERE AND I'LL BLOW IT OUT. He couldn't figure out why they left in a hurry. The men sitting around there told Charlie and everybody had a good laugh.

In the early 1960's, two young ladies showing more skin than had been seen before, stopped at Keith Skelly's station I Wheatland, for gas. While the car was being filled they asked, "are we in the Ozarks yet? And where can where see a hillbilly?" The reply was gentle and soft. "The first person you see when you drive south, that has clothes on...now that is a hillbilly."

It was Halloween night in the early 1950's. there was a group of younger boys and a group of older boys. The younger boys discovered the older boys jug of apple cider hid under the hotel porch in Wheatland. Without thinking, the five boys drank about half of the jug, then a light came on. One of the boys said when our older brothers find out we drank their cider, we will get the hell beat out of us. We will put water in the jug. One of the boys said that will turn it light color. Then after a little bit, we came up with a bright idea. To keep from getting the hell beat out of us. So we all relieved ourselves in that jug, till it was back to where it was, when we got it. Never did hear anything about that jug of cider.

Henderson Murphy has hair lipped and never married. At the age of 49 on hot day, he drove a herd of hogs to Wheatland to sell. When he got there, he was very hot and thirsty so he drank a lot of cold water. He became sick, got a room in the hotel. Someone later went to check on him and couldn't wake him. They ran to get the doctor, he was pronounced dead. The doctor said it looked like cholera. He was placed at once in a coffin and buried, even before notifying his kin. Year later, a young lady said that when she walked by the coffin, she could see sweat on his forehead. So frightened, she couldn't tell the doctor or grown men what she had seen. The lid was nailed shut and lowered into the grave. The young lady was so hysterical, she didn't tell this till years later.

Hickory county living, dying and people and their ways and economy:

When the land we now call Hickory county was first settled, there were several natives or Indians, as we call them, living here. The larges tribe was Osage. While sub tribes as Fox, Kiowa Cherokee and Weaubleau. Their lives were simple, but well stable. The Foxes were the largest in the county. Slowly pushed back across the west of Pomme de Terre river. This remained stable till about 1830. In the years before, this Hickory County as we know it now was a no man's land. Where the outlaws had free reign. Most of the land was very rough. Without the knowledge of living in this type of terrain, finding your way out could be very difficult. Just west of the river where Indians made camp, we can find large settlements remain and burial grounds. Some rock covered and some small mounds scattered over the fields and pasture. Paints or artifacts can be found about anywhere. Upon careful examination, villages can be located by a collection of rocks that have spent lots of time in a fire pit. The shelters were built out of poles in the ground covered with smaller poles. Cedar timber made good covering plus animal hides. Deer, elk, bison, bear, mountain lions, bobcats were very plentiful. Small game both for food and other articles needed for life. The rivers were very abundant in all types of water life.

As people kept moving west, slowly the land was being settled. Pittsburg was one of the first because of the large amounts of lead, zinc and barate discovered. Soon after come Garden City. Later to be named Cross Timbers. Black Oak Point later Preston, Goose Neck later Almon, children in the extreme northeast of the county no longer here, Lone Spring 4-1/2 miles southeast of Preston no longer here. Jordon east of Cross Timbers in some of the leased settled land. Roney, northeast of now where Hermitage is. The county area was a narrow strip between Benton and Polk counties.

The law at this time in History, you must be within a day's journey to get to the courthouse. To get to Warsaw, Bolivar or Buffalo, was a 4 day round trip. Three men net with the government of Missouri. Upon his order with Missouri congress a new county was to be formed. The designers took the largest part from Benton county and another large area from Polk. Smaller parts taken from St. Clair and Camden, to the shape it is today.

Life was hard, very primitive. Life had to be what came from the land. To exist, no law except your own. To get supplies could be 4 days away when first settlers.

Slowly it became easier to get supplies and exchange what the settler could harvest from the land, to trade for needed supplies. This type of life didn't begin to change till the early 1900 to late 1800.

For most settlers they must live off the land in one way or another. To me this is why the writing of Plainville USA viewed the people very illiterate and backward. The 2nd World War caused an unbelievable change in life style. Life in the country was pushed to take more products to the market as it was needed to help our war machine business. Then after the war was over, the men and women that had been included to outside world war, no longer were satisfied with just hard life in the hills.

People left their houses to move to the city. A new type of living was introduced to the country. We were now able to live on an upscale type of life.

Very few young boys and girls after graduation stayed close to home, but went to the brightest lights of the city.

Life on the farm also began to change in the late 1930. A horse carriage could be seen on occasion. The horse replaced the oxen for farm work. After the 2nd World War, an explosion came about in the rural communities. Cars and trucks were to be seen and a few tractors replacing the horse. One old timer stated they will never get them machines to do things a horse can't do and do it better. Electricity was being introduced by a coop by the name of REA, Rural Development Agency. With this women were able to have washing machines, refrigerators, deep freezes, running water, small appliances, and a host of other things to make life better. But these were a very large group that would have all of this but not lights in the house. For in a few years, it would cause you to go blind. The light bulb took a little longer to be accepted ad daily living.

Most of rural people made their income from milking. Most farmers were quick to buy a milking machine. So instead of six cows to milk, he could now handle 60. This increasing their standard of living. The farmers needed to do an economical job of farming. The supplies were very limited. Very little of a number of food items, which hurt the city folk a lot more if no garden was available. Farmers put up a lot of sorghum, honey to be used for sugar, large gardens to can a large supply of vegetables, meat both canned and salted and dried several wild life and fish were harvested in the winter.

After the war, machinery evolved more modern every year. So many people were leaving the agriculture way of life for a much easier life working in the city. The farmer bought more land and needed larger machinery. Every kind of machine anybody could think of was enlarged or a new kind was invented. The larger the farm was, the larger the equipment. As several farmers would remark each year, "going to have to make my gate wider". The tilling equipment went from 24 inches in width to 42 feet plus.

Grain harvesting also changed from harvesting by hand to a sled with a knife, to a binder for small grains and row crops. Threshing machines to corn pickers. Then combines to handle both small grains and row crops.

New types of crops were introduced, Milo, soy beans, canola, sunflower… they were also planted in large quantities.

Chemicals to keep insects and weeds away, also made it so the farmer could farm larger areas.

Plant breeding over the years, provided an explosion in the yield of crops. In 1940, it your corn made over 50 bu. per acre, you had a bumper crop. By 2014, if your corn don't make close to 200 bu. per acre, you don't make any money.

We read of test plots of 500 bu. per acre. Other grains have also gained dramatically in yield.

Milk productions are the same way. If you had a cow giving 9000 lbs. of milk a year, you were sitting in the kings row. Now if a cow doesn't give 40,000 lbs. in a year, you kill her.

Beef and hogs in the 40's and 50's and before were the main products for the fat. That changed dramatically in the late 50's and 60's. Now a hog is expected to reach 250 lbs. in 5 months, with very little to no fat. The calf is expected to weigh close to 500+ in 10 months with same breeds weighing a calf close to 1,000 lbs., no fat. They must display a good temperament.

The way the ground is prepare for planting, some use a chemical burn down, then no till and come back with week and disease spray. Very, very few farmers use full tillage any more. Some use what is called minimum tillage, where the soil is broken up on top and then plant grain into light worked soil, then chemicals are used for weeds and diseases.

To find a farmer or rancher that miss teats the soil or animals, is like looking for a needle in a hay stack. This is where the family living comes from and the better you treat your assets, the better they will treat you. I have never seen a farmer or rancher yet that doesn't leave things in better shape when he passes on than when he found it.

Now how putting up winter feed has changed. First we cut with a syth and cradle rake it up with a fork, load it on some kind of wagon, take it to the barn and pitch in hay loft with fork.

Then along came a horse drawn mower and a sulky rake, that put it in a windrow. From here we picked it up with a fork, hauled it to the barn or stacked it.

Then a auto hay stacker was invented, pulled by a horse. It brought hay close to stacks. Here an arm machine pulled by horses, picked up a huge cut and placed it in a loaf of bread like stack. Then the John Deere company invented a baler with a motor on it and one man on each side of bale chamber, poked wire through and tied it. Later it was figured out how to make a tractor pull it and pick it up from the windrow. In a short few years, the auto tying was invented for both string and wire.

In the 50's, Allis Chalmers tractor company, came out with a baler that made round bales, that weighed about 70-90 lbs. After this, we had an explosion in the inventing of haying equipment. The most dramatic being the large round bales. These cutting out requiring help to haul hay, which was getting very hard to find.

Most of today, workers don't require a 12-14 hour day, seven days a week. Time is taken off for community projects or fun for the family.

When you first sat up housekeeping in 1800 till 1900, all that was needed was desire to make it. Both husband and wife, when first married, could start a new life with very little resources. In today's economy or at least after the year 2000, to start out in agriculture without help from someone or family, it is impossible. A minimum of a $100,000 would be required plus long hours. The same goes to set a business in the city. Most couples work for someone else. Either way, most country folks are very stubborn or a nicer word independent. We like doing our own thing at our time schedule or at least so the natives of Hickory County. If when the city folk as we call them, settle down here in a few years, that independence rubs off them too. At that time, they are accepted as country folk. I won't go as far as to say Hillbillies for that would take some mighty strong change of attitude and way of life. This is the living part now, we will discuss the dying. Life in Hickory County has always been a subject to cherish. The bible states we should cry when a child is born and be joyful when one passes on from life. While this is true, we country folk mourn not for the dead, but for ourselves because we have lost a neighbor.

Maybe they lived several miles away and just knew of them. We mourn for the empty place left in our life. The same goes for the many types of livestock found in the country. The outsider might think those people are a little touched in the head. Several of the livestock have a name just like the human race. Sorrow is lift when livestock is sold, but when one gets sick or dies, then grief sets in. so explain the living and dying process in Hickory County. The greatest place on the earth to live and die.

Chapter 13

HICKORY COUNTY MEN WHO SERVED IN WORLD WAR I

The names listed below were sent to Ralph B. Nevins, Attorney at Law, by Monte C. Coulter, State Service Officer, State of Missouri, on February 28, 1936, in a response to Mr. Nevins' request for a complete list of Hickory Countians who served during World War I. Mr. Nevins volunteered to complete the paperwork for discharged veterans in the county.

Thanks go to Kathleen Liedtke, daughter of Ralph B. Nevins, for sharing this list with the Hickory County Recorder's Office, and to Vicky Stapleton, Hickory County Deputy Clerk, for sharing the list with us.

Question marks indicate name spellings that were not clear. Transcribed by Ginny Sharp, Nov. 2007.

Additional information on most of these men can be found on the Missouri Secretary of State's Website, Soldiers Database: War of 1812 - World War I.

NAME	ADDRESS
Allison, Jess	Wheatland
Anderson, Oscar	Cross Timbers
Ashcroft, Arthur P.	Weaubleau
Babcock, Olin H.	Weaubleau
Baldwin, Bert	Quincy
Bandel, Morris Albert	Hermitage
Bartshe, Duriel	Hermitage
Baxter, Charles	Gerster
Beets, Oliver	Wheatland
Beets, William C.	Wheatland
Bernard, Claud	Weaubleau
Beyer, William D.	Avery
Birdsong, Lester Dallas	Weaubleau
Blackwell, Clarence Edgar	Hermitage
Blackwell, Walter L.	Wheatland
Bliss, Perry P.	Cross Timbers
Boyle, Earl	Wheatland
Box, Earl H.	Wheatland
Brent, Dee	Quincy
Brent, Elmer R.	Quincy
Breshears, Roney F.	Avery
Brickey, Everett	Elkton
Bridges, Fred	Urbana
Britton, Harry	Wheatland
Brown, Ira L.	Almon
Buck, Gerald Emmitt	Elkton
Bybee, Harrison	Preston
Bybee, William H.	Preston
Cahow, John Oliver	Weaubleau
Chancellor, Thomas R.	Quincy
Clark, William Anderson	Pittsburg
Clonts, Weaver L.	Wheatland
Conkling, Frank	Avery
Coon, Raymond M.	Hermitage
Copeland, Boyd V.	Weaubleau
Cothern, Charles L.	Cross Timbers
Crawford, Oliver E.	Weaubleau
Crouch, Elbert Reid	Hermitage

Chapter 14

1860 HICKORY
COUNTY CENSUS

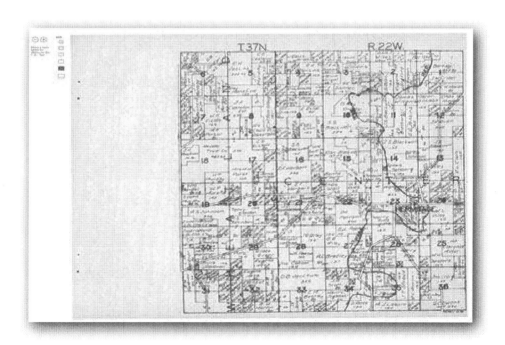

Bottom Left: Weaubleau, Mo., 1909. Left, Methodist Church, home, old grade school, Mary Sue Goans home, Christian Church which was the college then later grade school.

Chapter 15

CYCLONE OF 1917

On Friday, May 25, 1917, at 8:45 p.m., a cyclone struck the northwest corner of the Wheatland community and continued its destruction in a northeasterly direction. The path of the storm was about a hundred yards wide. Laying timber, giant trees and everything in waste as it moved on. The timber looked like a giant mover had run over them, many torn out by the roots. Straws and splinters were driven right into the trees.

Clouds began building up about 4:00 p.m. and the southwest sky was a dark and stormy picture. It attracted the attention of people in the neighborhood and a low rumbling sound could be heard in the distance. As it approached, the noise was louder. The lightning, keen and quick, was a greenish color.

It began by taking the roof off the barn at the present W.D. Thompson farm, then owned by Charlie Wright. It progressed across the next section to the Frank Bangle home where everything was blown away. The house and barn and other out buildings were torn into splinters. A sign of a building could be seen of the home site the next morning except part of a floor. A man's shoe was hanging from a tree limb. Mrs. Bangle was found sitting on a feather bed out in the timber east of where the house once stood. Mr. Bangle was found lying in a ditch across the road from the home site with water running over his body. It was thought he would have drowned in a short time. He was a large man, weighing between 250-300 pounds. He was ell of dropsy at the time and died the next year in June.

This location is where Guy and Mary Lee Foltz now live. The Maria Fine home was only a short distance away but there was no destruction there.

The Bangle's son, Lemon, was at home at the time with his parents. He was blown across the road and was unconscious or did not realize anything had happened until rain began to hit him in the face.

The Leonard Bangle family lived only about a half mile from his parents. He had built a new two room house and it was still unpainted. It was in the path of the storm. The wind carried it some distance and left it tumbled on its side.

They had a new dresser that had a glass broken into pieces. Several people picked up a piece and kept it as a souvenir. It was unusual glass for the time.

The Bangle family all had typhoid fever the next year and Mrs. Leonard Bangle (Callie Hostetler) died in August 1918. She left two children, a boy and girl.

Some chickens that survived were running around without any feathers on their bodies.

After the storm struck, Leonard's family started for his parents' home with the two children, the younger about two months. They were almost drowned when they reached the senior Bangles' home place and found everything gone. Those who were in the rain said there was never a harder rain fall.

The older Bangles had lost a daughter who lived only about six weeks after her marriage to Luke Forehand. She took typhoid fever and expired. She had been given a toilet set (mirror, brush and comb) by Luke before her marriage. Her things had been put in a trunk and looked for ten years. This vanity set was found in the Sumner cemetery. Some of the Bangles' pictures and papers were found in the woods.

The next house that was struck was Harry Bennett, about two miles north of Wheatland. Everything there was blown away except the house and smoke house. The barn located east of the house, was blown across the road a quarter of a mile away and scattered over the field. Berley Scarbrough, took his wagon and team and hauled the debris away before he could plow the field.

The Bennett had two rooms on the ground floor and an upstairs and a porch across the south. The house was moved eight foot off its foundation, every window pane was broken, every tree in the orchard was up rooted, and an apple tree was blown in at the window in the kitchen, and under the cook stove and lifted it up. The lamp which was lighted on a table in the living room, slid off on the floor and was extinguished, but did not break. Seth Bennett, a nephew, was in bed upstairs and slept through it all and was awakened by the excited family. They crawled out, one at a time through the window where the tree came in, to go to the cellar. Not a door could be opened. Cleo laid Helen then four months old, in one of the branches while she climbed out. The rain fell in torrents and the water was more than ankle deep in the yard. Not a shingle on the house, the beds were all wet, tables turned over, dishes on the floor, etc. Cleo had baked bread the day before and put her loaves in a big jar. She had strained three or four gallons of milk in crocks and set on the table. It had been upset into the jar of bread. The next day the loaves of bread were swelled up from being soaked in milk.

The children had a pet pig in ta good's box on the porch. When they began looking for it, it was found in the corner of the yard with the pig still in the box unhurt.

A mare and colt were in the pasture around the house, but next morning they were nowhere to be seen. About 11:00 a.m., Howard Crooks who lived about a mile and a half away came leading them home.

Cleo had 156 brown leghorn chicks; they found five of them. They also had between 300-400 hens. They picked up 146 dead ones.

Harry went to John Sherman's the next morning (now Garry Kragel's) and told them about the destruction and Mr. Sherman carried the message to Cleo's parents, Mr. and Mrs. H.W. Wente. They lived where Mr. and Mrs. Clifford Wetzel now live.

Mrs. Sherman was so nervous that Hobart and Lola played the organ and sang while to storm was raging.

The neighbors assisted the Bennett's to make the needed repairs and re-build their home.

This same storm hit with less force at the Luther Kelly place and moved the house and turned over the beehives. At the Bob Jenkins place, it took the rafters off the barn, they were building, and blew a sliver through the window over Alvin's bed.

CROSS TIMBERS TORNADO

A tornado struck Cross Timbers May 1, 1948. Considerable damage was done to buildings and trees. It came from the southeast. The terrific wind did damage to property of the following persons: Mitchell's store, Mrs. Anna Jenkins, J.C> Easterday, Tint and Bert Hickman, Ras Robertson, Frank Schnitker, Jack Fishback, Oral Bruton, W.E. Kugler, Tot Stevens, Mrs. Ada Coon, Mrs. Ida Rose, B.B. Scarbrough, L.H. Nance, J.A. Schooley, Larry Breshears, Homer Ames, B.H. Cothern, D.P. Ussery, John Crawford, and Marion Cothern. There were as many as 25 barns destroyed and many other smaller buildings. Only one person was injured, Miss Sharlene Thomas, who was struck by a falling timber. Several stitches were necessary.

TORNADO HITS AVERY, MISSOURI, JANUARY 1933

Homes in Breashears ancestral valley wrecked by storm. Violent wind dips prankishly into fertile region, crumpling houses, but injuring inhabitants only slightly.

Warsaw, Mo.–A tornado late Saturday, dipped into the Breshears ancestral valley to Avery, Missouri and wreaked homes rich in memories for the descendants of Henry Breshears. Only slight injuries were suffered by the inhabitants.

Henry Breshears moved from Tennessee in 1859 an set up his black smith shop in the valley at what is now known as Avery, Mo. Just off the Pomme de Terre branch of the Lake of the Ozarks and sixteen miles south of Warsaw. From the vigorous smith 500 Breshears descended and inhabited the valley.

Its fertile 6,000 acres are homed in on every side by hills. There is only one entrance. Fossils discovered in the valley bottom have indicated it was a wallowing place for prehistoric monsters. Mastodon bones have been found there.

AN 8 ROOM LOG HOME

Henry Breshears built his home of oak logs, wedged firmly together with wooden pins, two stories high and containing eight rooms. He built with the expectations of a family and built well. His expectations were fulfilled and other homes were built.

The home of Henry survived him and the ravages of deterioration and weather. With the advent of the saw mill, it had been clothed in lumber, which became weather beaten and belied somewhat the strength Henry had built, but the Breshears who were sheltered by its walls, felt its security.

It was said for many years that non-but a Breshears and his wife could dwell in the valley. The ownership of the land maintained the tradition largely, oven when a good road was built over a hill to admit motorcars. Even bad economic conditions little disturbed the security of the valley

Saturday the breath of spring was in the valley and late in the day it grew into the oppressive warmth and stillness that precedes summer thunderstorms. Clouds obscured the setting sun and light rain drove the inhabitants into their homes. A peculiar darkness enveloped the valley and the inhabitants turned in wonder to light lamps. Before they could accomplish their purpose, a trembling of their houses interrupted.

Lee Breshears, 65 years old, thought someone was knocking. He groped to the front door and opened it. A mighty force jerked it from his hand and slammed it shut. But he had had a glimpse of the destruction that was moving down the valley.

He turned and called to his wife and their 10 year old grandson, Jimmie Breshears, who were in the kitchen to escape from the house. They did, but he was caught as the house caved in upon him. Lee Breshears was dug from the wreckage, by men wielding axes. He had suffered only sever cuts on his head.

A short distance away the ancestral home built by Henry Breshears crumpled. Birchie Breshears, the present possessor, was in the home with his daughters, Mable, 18, and Helen and Ellen, twins, 12. J.A. Jones was a visitor on the front porch. Helen suffered a severe cut on her left leg. Jones was bruised badly by the falling roof of the porch. All the others were left standing uninjured in the wreckage.

A HOME CARRIED 20 FEET

The general store and the home of Mrs. Willie Breshears, its proprietor, were destroyed without injury to anyone. The home of Marion Breshears was picked up and carried 20 feet from its foundation, with only the breaking of a window. A mattress was sucked through the broken window and deposited on a tree nearby without suffering a tear.

No one could remember any definite sound accompanying the phenomena. The action was as fast that most of the inhabitants remember only a transition from peace to chaos.

An old spinning wheel found about 50 yards from the Marion Breshears home standing as though ready to work.

The pat of the storm was about 100 yards wide and ten miles lone. It did not deal complete destruction in that path, however, rather picking here and there prankishly.

NAMES REGISTERED BY TOWNSHIPS— WORLD WAR II

TUESDAY, JUNE 5, 1917

CENTER TOWNSHIP

Amos Downs, George Emory Wilson, Ora Hollingsworth, James Melvin Wright, Isaac Wesley Clark, Charlee O. Skinner, Silas Luther Kelley, Perry C. Penny, Benjamin Harrison Brakebill, Rolland Houston Amlin, Hubert Roy Moreland, Everett Marvin Austin, Clarence Lloyd Miller, Grover Cleveland Stroud, Noel Frank Huffman, Walter Homer Boyd, Leslie Jacob Chaney, Clyde Edwin Dorman, John R. Kelley, George W. King, George W. Donovan, Elon Blackwell, Thomas I. Jordan, Clarence E. Wilson, Ernest Guy Martin, Oral J. Bartshe, Albert Roy Hinkle, John Wesley Stout,

Edward Heath, Archie Lovel Miller, Elmer D. Coon, Harry Pitts, Daniel H. McGee, William H. Sutt, John E. Eidson, Dee Blair, ? Johnson, Aaron Cowen, John William Rash, James Draper Herbort, John Leonard Holland, Alvin S. Jenkins, Arthur Smith Jones, Weaver Lee Clontz, Joseph Ross Johnson, Harmon C. Jenkins, Joseph Claude Pearson, Daniel Bartshee, Ralph F. Wilson, James Asa Losure, John Albert Foltz, Charles Luther McCain, Walter Andrew Parkhurst, Charles James Solberg, Edward Peter Peterson, Perry Wiley Darby, Sylvester Pearson.

STARK TOWNSHIP

George Washington Mitchell, Ancel Edwin Erickson, William Henry Bybee, Homer C. Hurt, George Washington Owsley, Elmer Erickson, Jim Stirlen, Charlie Landreth, Arnold Jackson, Burnie Dorrel Baldwin, Roy L. Edde, Harrison Hobert Bybee, John Henry Anderson, Roy Ernest Marsh, Garland Godfrey Bandel, Garrett Marion Russell, Charles Leslie Green, Arthur Ernest Erickson, Ezra D. Parrack, Elwood Franklin Scott, Ira L. Brown, Edward Hall, Robert Parker Cross, Charles B. Hart, Francis E. Erickson, Willie K. Whittenburg, Willia Robert Wile, Ernest Lee Erickson, Archiblad C. Odenbaugh, Homer Harrison King, Pearl A. Warner, John O. Hires, Luther James Palmer, Robert Elmer Howard, Richard W. Phillips, Timothy Lake, Henry Ruby McCain, Lucinous McCoy, Joseph William Ussery, Jacob Roscoe Stroud, James Marion Dalton, George Albert Bandel, George Franklin Mabary, Thomas S. Morgan, Floyd Edgar Green, Frank Stirlon, Arlie Jackson, Arthur Lake, Jasper Wheeler Parrack, Kinley Glemons, Homer Lea, James Franklin McCain, Leo Peral Canon, Jasper Earl Philbert, Lewis Whittenburg, Horea Sales Climons, Guy Clester Marsh, John H. Edde, George G. Mabary, Ernie Addison Baldwin, Elmber Ernest Hollingsworth, Loren Donaldson Green, Odus Walker, William Ray Howard, William D. Jackson, Floy Edgar Walker, James Shorman Bybee, Bandel Edde, Harry A. Johnson, William Erby Riddle, Elijah William Bray, Roscoe Edde.

GREEN TOWNSHIP

Herman Cethcart Johnson, John Clifford Case, Faronco Russell McBride, William Fritz Allen Reed, Arthur Newcomb, James Elbert Fisher, James Andrew Taylor, Claude Glanville, Guy Berkley Duncan, Omer Sigel Fisher, James Henry Williams, Fred Bridges, Griffie Pitts, Lowell Crawford Lowe, Douglas Loren Reed, Robert Ingersoll Russell, Roy Laurel Rush, Alfred Houston Williams, Samuel Julian Sargent, Elmer Thomas Pitts, Andro Floyd, Romey Fowler, Henry Elmer Kelley, Wilbur Glanville, Roy Williams, John Alvin Kelley, Elmer Martin Fugate, Oscar Oliver Sapp, Willie Everett Davis, Fleming August Taylor, Isaac Brantley Bush, Edward Sutton, Soloman Erby Carter, Levi Rimbey, Ike Buckner, Roy Shaw, James Thompson, John Ceal Baker, Wiley Valentine Bonner, Evert Pitts, Lee Hicks, Roy Davis, Benjamin Harrison Landroth, Benjamin Lyon Mallonee, Harry Dell Smith, Benjamin Harrison Reser, Weslie Newton Nelson, Cecil Lodell Walker, William Alfred Brown, Earl Roscoe Lindsey, Joseph Warner Lopp, Charley Guy Kincaid, Eugene E. Clymore, Benjamin Franklin Crawford, Charles Franklin Nelson, Freeman D. Lightfoot, John Elgin Whittenburg, Roberty Raymond Simmons, Daniel Aaron Larose, Noah Winfrey Frazier, Jesse Toliver, John Thomas Welch, Arvie Leslie Dorman, Thomas Earl Ferguson, Charley Christopher Pitts, John Earl Pitts,, William Don Belknap, Arcie Pitts, William Ransom Garner.

TYLER TOWNSHIP

Clifford Oliver Aspey, Oscar James Rupard, Leroy Benton Selvidge, Charley Lenard Harris, Zifa Otto McCracken, Bert Green, Ormel Christopher Williamson, Fred Daniel Miller, John Parker Harris, Albert Enis Blackwell, Francis Marion Stewart, Samuel Russell Harrison, Rolla Howard Luse, James Orlie Vaughn, Ethmer Clyde Gothmer Fisher, Jesse Matthew Kelly, Lester Dorman, Claud Lawrence Dunivant, Charley Preston Boren, George William Cyrus, Oliver Ernest Blackwell, Inmon Newton Hofstetter, Robert Frederick Berg, Roy Lydorgus Vaughn, Asa Roy Tinsley, John Thorton Morton, Edgar Elbert Delozier, Willis Dumford Niblack, Frank Edward Hellums, Charley Liben Walters, Charley Homer Cauthen, Walter

Roy Edmondson, Gustavis Houston Babb, Elmer Hoses Oesch, Ross Alexander, Rufus Cleveland Parker, Andy Luther Cooper, Richard Orville Newport, Melvin Banister Lightfoot, John Samuel Hofstetter, William Frank Ward, Cody Carson McCracken, Earl Boyle, James Lowell Harris, Carlos Rupard McCracken, Arthur Fellers, Ralph B. Nevins, Clyde Coleman McCaslin, James Otis Poe, Ross Walker Morton, Limuill Roundtree.

WHEATLAND TOWNSHIP
Charles William Wright, Sherman A. Lindsey, Steve Mullins, John Clyde Woodward, Harry Britton, Woodson Newman Heard, William Clyde Beets, George Vernon Wright, Logan Britton, Harry Oral Largent, Charles Otis Gardner, John Lacy Norton, Thomas Wright, Leonard Heard, Leonard V. Martin, Wayland Pratt Gardner, Jesse Allison, James Franklin Lurten, Lemuel Ira Gist, Orville J. Paxton, Fred Gist, John Isaac Weaver, Ollie Goldman Breshears, John Albert Jenkins, David Ray Owsley, Henry Hadewell, John James Paxton, Buel Byron Ihrig, Carlos Clinton Crawford, Harry Edgar Bartshe, William Fred Bangle, Ernest Joseph Paxton, Seth Thomas Cogle, William Otto Bailey, Willie Daniel Thompson, Oliver Leo Jordan, George William Breshears, William Arnel Groves, Thomas Marion Groves, Leo Rupard, Elvin Milton Lacy, Carl Webster Allen, John Fred Cook, John Howard Crooks, Benjamin Hansen Romesburg, William Homer Jones, Clyde Estelle Holland, Orval Rife, Berley Washington Scarbrough, John Washington Thompson, William Leslie Pine, Claud Claborn Thompson, Leonard McKinley Bangle, Lomon Reed Bangle, Albert Hugh Paxton, Alvin Richard Kittel, Roy Lester Holland, Coy Edward Nutt, Buell Roy Breshears, William Raymond Paxton, George Greenwood Paxton.

MONTGOMERY TOWNSHIP
Thomas Claude McCaslin, Arley Brownlea Robinet, James Ward Allen, Otto Baster, Harry Wilber Myers, Elmer Ray Brent, Clyde Parish, Chas. Edward Selvidge, Harrell B. Sherman, Pete Roth, Edgar Allen Lacy, Luther Homer

Koele, Arthur Henry Ramsey, Thos. Edgar Bailey, Waldo Hemphill, Benjamin Franklin McCaslin, Roy David Miller, Jesse Feaster, Oscar Parsons, Perry Parke, Worden Hemphill, Evry Oval Shaw, William Ross Southard, Henry Howard Walker, Latham Adcock, William W. Hogsett, Claud Dietz, Herbert A. Page, Frank J. Tuck, James Iiams, Thomas R.F. Chancellor, Henry D. Chancellor, Raleigh E. Welch, Louie D. Thompson, Adam H. Bangle, Oscar D. Swopes, Harvey Jessie Miller, Joe Henry Melton, Ray Durnell, Noah Sylvestor Allen, Fred William Norton, John S. Allen, Walter Edwards Rains, Arthur Boone Moore, John Fredrick Lawson, Bert Harrison Durnell, John Larenzo Lazezzi, Hugh Jeffrey, Frank Stokes, Charles Orlie Vaughn, David Franklin Keeling, James Roy Coffey, Joseph Ernest Kittel, Thomas Lafayette Reno, Howard Stewart Ware, Stanley Goodson, Lester Dallas Birdsong, Morris Valentine Daniele, Claud Bernard, Arthur Putnam Ashcroft, Oliver Edward Comfort.

CROSS TIMBERS TOWNSHIP

Charles Logan Cothern, Elvin Harris Nance, Aaron Floid Sanford, Earl Vessie Wright, James Summer Guier, Ralph Thomas Stewart, Robert Samuel Smith, Arlandor Carl Stevens, Jesse Thomas Miller, Robert Johnson Cooper, Jacob Elmer Logan, Secanda Lloyd Pack, Benjamin Franklin Jenkins, Emory Miller, Abrum Mitchell, Malcham Dont Dickerson, George Albert Kugler, William Hayes Gist, Elmer Frederick Nelson, Roscoe William Bliss, Harrison Miller Harvey, Ezra Nance, Irl Rogers Chrisope, Benjamin H. Cothern, John Quincy Crawford, Leslie Earl Dickerson, John Henry Drenon, George Henry Thomas Hart, Ira Logsdon, James Robert Walthall, Evart Burr Wilson, Powers Ola Foltz, Heard Martin, John Walter Nelson, James William Demois, William Blueford Smith, Delmer Roy Breshears, William Roy Mawhiney,

William Alfred Drenon, Clarence Otis Little, Thomas Elmer McCarty, John Allen Demois, John Clifford McCarty, Ralph Clifford Gregory, Philip Andrew McFarland, Robert Everett Breshears, Charles Marion Drenon, William Arthur Mawhiney, Bertie Barnett Scarbrough, Remie A. Taylor, John Larence Nance, William Homer Hart, James Eddie Prine, Bengiman E. Rose.

Chapter 16

Some of the slang or words not used regular any more than one time was
regular in the Ozarks

Poke–paper bag; Bumfuzzel–don't understand or mixed up; Head in
the stars–don't see things in reality; Smell like pole cat–stink; Loose
cannon–lose temper to easy; Live in a pig pen–very dirty living; Not
worth their salt–good for nothing; Ants in their pants–can't sit still;
Thunk–think, Live on the back forty–backward; A joint–place where
you live; High on the hog–living and eating good; Spunk– try about
any task; Scratch your head–think; Sharper than a two edge sword–very
smart; Dumb as a turkey–very, very dumb; Cool–cold; Dumb as an ox–
has some learning yet to do; Sly as a fox–cunning; Just like a jackass–nice
way of saying bullheaded and stubborn; Yonder–a place way over there;
Fiddlesticks–I don't believe it; Over there a piece–just go that way; From
the frying pan to the fire–out of one mess to another; Welp–unruly
child; Howdy–hi; Two shakes of a sheep's tail–in a hurry; Gee–turn left;
Hau–turn right; Got spunk–he will try; Caught in cookie jar–guilty;
Hillbilly– outside in hills, very dumb, clothes very ragged; White lighten-
aged, moonshine; Moonshine–right out of the still; Caboust–in jail; Living
right–as the Lord would have; Hogwash–don't believe it; Bussile–large

butt; Gay–happy; Bird brain–not very smart; Pulling our leg–telling wild stories; Dumb as an ox–stubborn about believing; Yarns–big tales; Pulling my leg–trying to get me to believe; Furners–not from the Ozarks; Bullheaded–won't listen to reason; Watche–what you have; Then thar– them other people; Learned–had some schooling; Shoot the eyes out of a squirrel–very good shot; stout as an ox–very strong; hep–lot of something; We-uns–all of us; Burr under his saddle–edgy; Panties in a wad–out of sorts, cranky; Fixin'–getting ready to go; Fix-ins–have what needed to fix a meal; Pie in the sky–dreamer; Shucks–a by word meaning hard to be- lieve; Fetch–bring; Coke–drink; Pad–paper to write on; Sowbelly–bacon; Skunk oil–treatment for a cold; Not a lick of horse sense–not in real- ity; Loose cannon–very quick and hot temper; Froe to rive–four to five; Yep–I understand; Put that in your pipe and smoke it–how do you like that; Hogwash–lies; Bull shit–not true; Got the bull by the tail–things are going my way; Hog wild–went crazy; Loose cannon–cannot control the tongue; Pissed off–mad; Redneck–backward; Redneck peckerwood– a lack of good sense; John–toilet; Two bits–twenty five cents; Four bits– fifty cents; Six bits–seventy five cents; Toad strangler–very heavy rain; Eating high on the hog–living very good; A polecat–lowdown person; Don't give a hoot–couldn't care less; Shucks–don't bother me; Bull in a china shop–very clumsy; Whippersnapper–know it all, smart a lick; Hock it–loan for money; Fer–for you; Far–over there a piece.

REFERENCES

Plainville U.S.A.
Plainville Revisited
Notes from Geraldine Bird (Breshears)
Notes from Tom Sanders (written as quoted by Faye Allen and Nannie Jenkins)
Research from Hickory County Library
Bob and Oma Dickerson
Stories from old timers not with us anymore

Made in the USA
Columbia, SC
10 August 2019